Hampshire Heroes

Volunteer Fighters in the Spanish Civil War

by Alan Lloyd

The Clapton Press

Hampshire Heroes: Volunteer Fighters in the Spanish Civil War

© 2022 Alan Lloyd

Cover by Gruffydd Design

First published 2022 by:
The Clapton Press Limited
38 Thistlewaite Road, London E5

ISBN: 978-1-913693-18-3

Contents

Acknowledgements

Despite being involved in the Labour and Trade Union movement, and interested in history, all my life, it was not until about fifteen years ago when I bought William Rust's book 'Britons in Spain', that I realised that not only did men from my local area of Southampton and Portsmouth fight in Spain, but a number died there as well.

I then determined to find out about them and to write their stories, so they would receive the recognition they thoroughly deserved. The original half a dozen names has grown to around forty from across Hampshire and the Isle of Wight. Finding out about them has involved contacting over one hundred relatives, friends, librarians and archivists across the world. It has involved village history societies, Local Authority libraries and record offices, the invaluable International Brigade Archives in the Marx Memorial Library (MML) in London, the Russian State Archive of Socio-Political History (RGASPI) in Moscow and the Tamiment Library in New York.

I would also like to offer my sincere thanks to everyone who has been so helpful and patient in trying to answer my, often, persistent questions, when trying to fill in the all the details of each life. It is impossible to try and name everyone, so please accept this as a sincere thank you. The only name I will mention is that of the legend that was Jim Carmody. Jim was the go-to person for so many years when it came to answering questions about the members of the British Battalion, and I could never have made even a start of this project without his help. He continues to be sadly missed.

During the research for the book, we also fund-raised and erected a permanent memorial to the four lads connected to Southampton who were killed, and rediscovered Jimmy Moore's grave in Milton Cemetery, Portsmouth, which now has an appropriate headstone. I thank everyone who was involved, or contributed towards making these memorials happen.

Every effort has been made to attribute photographs and reference quotes correctly. Any errors or omissions are mine alone and I will be happy to apologise and correct them in any future edition. Finally, a massive thank you to my wife, Beth Richards, for all the unwavering help, support and encouragement she has given me.

It has been a very long, but satisfying journey to produce this book, which I hope is a fitting testimony to those who went to Spain.

THIS MEMORIAL IS DEDICATED TO
THOSE MEN OF THE INTERNATIONAL BRIGADES
FROM SOUTHAMPTON,
WHO GAVE THEIR LIVES IN BATTLE FIGHTING
FOR DEMOCRACY IN SPAIN (1936-39)

RAYMOND ARTHUR COX	BOADILLA DEL MONTE	DECEMBER 1936
HAROLD LAWS	SEGURA DE LOS BANOS	FEBRUARY 1938
DAVID HADEN GUEST	GANDESA	JULY 1938
IVOR RAE HICKMAN	EBRO	SEPT 9EP

"YOU ARE HISTORY, YOU ARE

Introduction

The coup d'état which began in Spain in July 1936, and was labelled as the 'Spanish Civil War', was the precursor to World War Two. It proved to be a valuable testing ground for Nazi Germany and Fascist Italy, using new weapons and tactics which were later deployed across the rest of Europe and other parts of the world. The fascist leader of the rebels, General Franco, was able to utilise massive amounts of men and equipment, particularly planes and heavy artillery, from Germany and Italy.

In contrast, the democratically elected Spanish Republican Government was constrained by the so called 'Non-Intervention Treaty' concocted by the 'Great Democracies' of Britain, USA and France. This was used as an excuse to falsely claim the conflict was purely a Spanish issue and meant that, contrary to international law, the Republican Government were prevented from buying arms and equipment on the open market, a travesty which was ultimately to prove decisive. The only countries to stand with Spain were the Soviet Union and, to a much lesser extent, Mexico.

However, the Spanish Government did receive the support of over 35,000 men and women, from over 50 countries across the world, who recognised the evil of fascism and the danger to the world it presented, and who were prepared to die in Spain to prevent its spread. They included almost 2,500 from Britain and Ireland, of whom over 520 would never return home. Most came from the big industrial and commercial centres of South Wales, the North East, Scotland, London, Manchester, but all parts of the UK and Ireland were represented. This included around 40 men and women connected to the County of Hampshire who participated as soldiers, doctors, nurses or pilots, and it is their stories I have attempted to tell in this book.

Having researched these men and women over the past 15 years, I believe their backgrounds and politics are fairly representative of all the British and Irish volunteers who went to Spain, but each of their stories is unique and provides a fascinating insight into the times they lived through.

Readers may notice that I have stretched the boundary of current day Hampshire to include Bournemouth and the Isle of Wight, simply to ensure that stories of people from these areas are also told.

This book does not attempt to explain the many complexities of the Spanish Civil War or the details of the major battles. There are many good books available which cover these aspects in great depth, some of which I have recommended in the notes. However, I hope readers will find it possible to follow the main events of the war through the stories of the individual Hampshire volunteers.

This book is dedicated to them and their International and Spanish comrades. Their cause was just, and their example a shining one in the battle against fascism which, regrettably, continues to this day.

Chapter One

July-December 1936—The Coup Begins, and Early International Arrivals

The Spanish General Election in February 1936 was a tremendous triumph for the left wing coalition, the Popular Front. Consisting of a host of parties, including Socialists, Republicans, Catalan and Basque separatists, and Communists, the coalition set about implementing a radical agenda, which included basic education for all and land reform. Having enjoyed the benefits of a near feudal system for centuries, this was not something the ruling class were ever going to easily accept, and the plotting of a coup d'état began immediately.

On 17/18 July 1936 the uprising began. Led initially by General Emilio Mola it started in Morocco and the Spanish peninsula, with a brutality that was to symbolise the fascist regime for decades. Anyone opposing the action, including several Generals, were summarily executed. However, the coup leaders had badly underestimated the anticipated public support for their actions. Loyal army units, and militias organised by the large Anarchist movement and Trade Unions, quickly sprang into action and subdued early attempts to remove the elected Republican Government.

The coup attempt was clearly failing, and was only saved when desperate pleas for assistance to Hitler and Mussolini were answered with a fleet of transport aircraft bringing the Spanish Army of Africa across the Strait of Gibraltar into Andalusia to form a bridgehead.

By the end of September General Franco had been made leader of the coup and declared himself to be head of the Spanish state. Under his leadership the fascists began their advance on Madrid, thinking they would enjoy a quick success and bring the coup to an early end.

Meanwhile France prohibited the delivery of arms to the Republican Government and, in London, the 'Non-Intervention' Committee met for the first time. However, many thousands of men and women across the world were not prepared to stand back and allow a fascist coup, and began the journey to Spain from which so many would not return.

Early arrivals in Spain attached themselves to the various militias which had been formed, particularly for the defence of Madrid. However, in October 1936 the International Brigades were formed, with the British having enough numbers to form their own Battalion in January 1937.

Robert Arthur Symes (1905-1936)

'Ronnie' Symes was born on 12 June 1905 in Keynsham, Somerset. His father, Arthur, was a general produce merchant who died just two years later, days after the birth of his younger brother. The family must have been well provided for, as Ronnie was a boarder at The College, in Newton Abbott, in 1921. He and his widowed mother then made a trip to Kenya in 1927 and, in 1929-33, he made three other trips to South America, with his occupation given as either farmer or agriculturist, with addresses in Somerset.

There is no positive Hampshire address for Ronnie when he went to Spain, but in 1939 his mother was living in the rural area of Michelmersh, Hampshire, and brother Arthur was the manager of the Merchant Navy Club in Southampton.

No records have been found to explain why he went to Spain, nor any evidence of any political allegiances. However, he arrived in Spain in October 1936, and joined the Commune de Paris Battalion of the XI International Brigade.[1] They were soon moved up to support the defence of Madrid, with the resultant action being documented by John Sommerfield, Jan Kurzke and Alfred Kantorowicz.[2] [3] [4]

There was a call for men experienced on Lewis guns to take the forward position in the Casa de Campo, the wooded area in front of University City. Ronnie, along with New Zealand born Cambridge graduate Griffith Maclaurin,[5] active London communist Steve Yates, and former British Army soldier Joe Hinks,[6] who was later to command the British Battalion, were accompanied by a largely French company of infantry. On 9 November 1936 they came under a heavy attack from a large force of Moroccan Moors, Franco's shock troops. The Lewis gunners stayed behind to cover the retreat, and only Joe Hinks was to escape alive.

Another Cambridge graduate, Communist intellectual and poet, John Cornford, who was also killed just a few weeks later, said of those killed in that action, 'It's always the best seem to get the worst'.[7]

Raymond Arthur Cox (1914-1936)

Ray Cox, was born in Reading on 25 May 1914—and died in the Castilian village of Boadilla del Monte, fifteen miles west of Madrid, 700 miles from Southampton, on the 15th of December 1936, at the age of twenty-two.[8]

Born four years after his elder brother Nick, their father, Sydney Herbert Cox, died trying to rescue workmates after a catastrophic explosion in a munitions factory in Faversham, Kent, that killed over a hundred men and women in February 1916.[9] This left their mother, Emily Florence—Flo—née O'Keeffe, to bring up her sons on her own. She scorned the plan of the local authorities to move her, sons and all, into the workhouse. Eventually she remarried, to Cecil Frank Wadge—known as Jack. They never had children, but he up brought her two sons as if they were his own. The brothers attended Faversham Grammar School, but both left at fourteen, because although they were bright boys, times were hard, and higher education was not for the poor.

By May 1933 the family had moved to Flat 4, 28 Highfield Lane, Southampton, and Ray was working for Brazier & Son building contractors as a wages clerk. The testimonial they wrote on 24 September 1936, says that he had 'marked ability', possessed initiative, and 'has proved himself thoroughly trustworthy in every respect'. Both brothers joined the Communist Party, and Ray also joined the Clarion Cycling Club whose Southampton section he co-founded, and where he was known as 'Tommy'.[10] He was also an active member of the Shop Assistants Union and Southampton Trades Council.

When Ray sailed from Southampton to Le Havre on his way to Spain, his mother waved goodbye from the dockside, and it was reported in the local newspaper that she felt she wouldn't see him again. Prior to going he had told her and his brother that he 'had a call to go and assist the democratic government of Spain in their fight for liberty, and that by fighting for the Spanish Government against the forces of Fascism I shall be helping preserve peace throughout Europe, because if the Spanish Government win the war it will mean that a European conflict will be further off.'[11]

When he reached Barcelona he joined up with an English group called the Tom Mann Centuria—eighteen men, too few to form a unit of their own.[12] They trained for a few weeks in Barcelona, and voted to join the Thaelmann Battalion of the XII International Brigade, which made them welcome.[13] These were Germans, a hard bunch with some serious political history behind them as part of the opposition to Adolf Hitler's Nazi Party which had been in power since 1933. Some of them were graduates of the early concentration camps.

An account of Ray's group, called 'Boadilla', was written by

Esmond Romilly, who joined the Centuria around this time and stayed with it to the end.[14] He noted that Ray Cox was 'patently nice and helpful . . . Everyone liked Ray, or rather, to show how *really* popular he was, no one disliked him.' He also quoted Ray's intervention to stop a really serious dispute inside the group: 'Comrades, we *must* stop this quarrel.' This view of Ray was confirmed by Keith Scott-Watson who wrote, 'Ray Cox was an enthusiast and remained one to the end. Ray's optimism never allowed a murmur . . . Things were always "fine". An office clerk and a Party member, he was a personal plea for the un-Marxian doctrine of mind over matter.'[15] He was elected as secretary/treasurer of this small group and kept a meticulous record of the accounts, which were largely their meagre pay as income, and the outgoings mainly telegrams home, and tobacco if they could find any.[16]

With Franco's forces pushing to capture Madrid, the Thaelmann Battalion was thrown into bitter fighting south-east of the city and near the university. Eight of the original eighteen British men were killed. Ray wrote to tell his brother: 'A hell of a lot of fine guys have gone west.' Ray's notebook entry for 24 November states, 'Kari wounded & died later—dum-dum.' 30 November: 'In line. Hans Beimler dead.'

On the morning of 14 December the Thaelmann and Dabrowski battalions were moved to the village of Boadilla del Monte, west of Madrid, where a rebel attack was expected.[17] They were surrounded, outnumbered, caught in cross-fire. Romilly's last sight of Ray 'was sitting in front of a tree firing when he crumpled up and collapsed . . . That night the commander took the roll-call: "Addley . . . Avner . . . Birch . . . Cox . . . Gough . . . Jeans . . . Messer . . ." No reply. Entered as *gefallen*. His body was never recovered.'

Ray's death came as a great shock in Southampton, both because he was so popular and also because he was the first local casualty of the war. Among the letters of condolence received by his mother were those from Braziers, his former employer, the local Regent Cycling Club, and the Southampton and National Branches of the Clarion Cycling Club. At their meeting on 6 January 1937, Southampton Trades Council passed the following emergency resolution, 'This Council expresses its admiration of the courage of our late Colleague Brother R A Cox of the Shop Assistants Union, in going to assist the Democratic Government of Spain in their fight against the fascist rebels. It deeply regrets his passing and expresses its deepest sympathy with Mrs Cox in the great loss she has suffered by his death.'[18]

Southampton Trades Council subsequently organised a collection in memory of Ray, which was extended after the death Of Harold Laws. Enough was raised to supply equipment, to administer anaesthesia, to the International Military Hospital of Ontinyent, which was close to Valencia.

On 26 January 1937 a memorial meeting in Ray's honour was held in the Connaught Hall, Southampton. It was organised by the Southampton Section of the National Clarion Cycling Club, and amongst those present were his mother and brother, and men and women in their cycling kit. The Trade Union and Labour Movement were also there in numbers headed by Alderman Tommy Lewis, the Leader of Southampton Labour Party, and Ralph Morley who gave the main address.[19] [20] He said that Ray had 'died fighting not only for the freedom of his own country but for the freedom of mankind . . . He had lost his life in the struggle against Fascism, which despised life, but glorified death, war, and mass slaughter.'[21]

The combination of the early international arrivals like Ray and Ronnie, and their loyal Spanish comrades, meant that Madrid was saved from the fascist advance. The front lines around the capital hardly moved during the whole of the war, and Madrid was never taken in battle.

Ray Cox outside his Highfield Road home
Courtesy of Steve Cox

Chapter Two

The Pilots

The most immediate problem facing the Spanish Government after the coup began was the lack of pilots. The majority of the officer corps, who tended to come from the Spanish ruling class, deserted to the fascists. The Government's temporary solution to this was to offer lucrative contracts to foreign aviators whilst they trained their own pilots. This meant that most of the foreign pilots who supported the Government were mercenaries and so, unlike the International Brigaders, they fought for money. However, the price they paid in return was a high one.

Edward Gawin Downes-Martin (1909-1936)

Edward Downes-Martin was born on 19 May 1909, in Teddington, Middlesex. He born into a very privileged life as a result of the efforts of his great grandfather, John Martin of Killyleigh, who had owned the largest cotton, and later flax, mill in Shrigley, Ireland. The fortune earnt by the mill allowed John Martin to purchase Shrigley Hall, and later Killoskehane Castle in Tipperary, and Edward's father, also called Edward, was the High Sheriff of County Tyrone for a period.

By the time of Edward's birth the family had sold the vast estate and decamped to England where they made their home in 'Avonmouth House' in Mudeford, near Christchurch, now in Dorset.[22] Edward snr died in 1924, leaving Edward a significant sum which he spent on various ventures, beginning with a cruise around the Canary Islands in 1925. He also purchased 'Avon Wharf' in Christchurch and sought to establish a boat yard there. In July 1932 he married professional ice skater Lily Morley at the Parish Church in Christchurch. Just prior to marrying he had learnt to fly at the Wiltshire School of Flying at High Post Airfield near Salisbury, and obtained his private pilot's license.

According to his local paper he was 'always of an adventurous turn of mind' and he had 'thrilled Christchurch on more than one occasion, and his name became associated with dare devil escapades.'[23] One such stunt came when he had flown off on honeymoon without filing a flight plan, and there were fears the couple had been lost. However it turned out that they had merely 'dropped in on France' for a while, which he alone considered a 'great joke'. The adventures continued when, two years later, he and some friends set off from Poole Harbour in a 20 foot yacht, which got as far as Vigo in Spain before they somehow managed to burn the boat out.[24]

In mid-August 1936 Edward decided to go to Spain, leaving his home in 'The Martens', Christchurch. His widow later explained that 'he was just fed up with hanging about the house with nothing to do. He has never had a job, always had enough money, and that bored him sometimes'.[25] Rather prophetically, he said to Lily as he left that he hoped 'it's a nice death. If I have to die, and it does seem possible, I don't want it to be agony. I would rather have it that way than you having to meet me in pieces at Waterloo.'

He arrived at the aerodrome at Getafe, Spain, after leaving London on 7 September a few days after Claude Warsow. On 25 September he was one of three Nieuport Ni-D.52s escorting a flight of bombers on the Toledo front when they were attacked by six Fiat CR.32s. One was quickly on Edward's tail, and an explosive bullet in the back of his neck sent him plunging to earth.

Fellow British pilots, Charles Kenneth and Patrick Mertz claimed the outcome was inevitable saying, 'All we had in the way of machines were old fashioned and clumsy Martinsyde fighters, whereas the other side had 1936 Heinkels and Fiats, piloted by regular air trained men. We simply hadn't a chance. In our first raid we lost two planes, for some of our number were practically raw airmen and the machines were museum pieces'.[26] Edward clearly did not share their downbeat assessment. Lily noted how she had received his final letter just a few days before this death, and said that 'he was as usual very bright, and said that all the Englishmen kept together and were having a really happy time in spite of the war . . . He was bound to die like this. I knew it all the time. It is well I have no children. I can go on working'.[27]

Edward Downes-Martin
Courtesy of the Royal Aero Club Trust

Claude Warsow (1903-1936)

Claude Warsow was born in Southsea, Portsmouth on 9 October 1903 the youngest of five children. His father, Joshua, was a cigarette maker, born in Constantinople, who enjoyed possession of a 'Warrant of Appointment' as a supplier to the Prince of Wales.[28] The family surname of Warshawski was anglicized shortly after Claude's birth to Warsow. After an education at St Helen's College, Portsmouth, he gave the appearance of being a man indulged by his parents and struggling to find a useful role in life, an example of which resulted in a court appearance for 'dangerous driving in a fast sports car'.[29] [30]

A degree of stability came when he signed up for a short-term commission in the RAF on 6 January 1926, although he still managed to get involved in the odd scrape, such as colliding with a milkman's horse and cart.[31] [32] Most of his five year commission was spent in the Middle East flying de Havilland DH9A's, and the final stint spent in the UK flying a twin-engine biplane day bomber.[33] His commission came to an end in January 1931, when he was transferred to the Reserve List.[34] Although, for some unknown reason this only lasted until October 1932, when he was removed from the List altogether.[35]

Having managed to escape a charge of drink driving shortly after leaving the RAF, he took a trip to the Bahamas in August 1931, claiming on the passenger list to be a 'playwright'.[36] On his return he was sued by a garage in the Hampshire village of Liphook for failure to pay a car repair bill.[37] He married Sybil Corbin, the daughter of a Portsmouth boot and shoe dealer, at the prestigious Caxton Hall Registry Office in London and then took over as the proprietor of the Passfield Oak Hotel in the New Forest village of Bramshott.[38] This may have been an attempt at trying to settle down, but if that was the case it was doomed to failure. By the time his daughter, Stephanie, was born in December 1935 the couple had already separated, and he had clocked up another appearance in court for driving offences whilst working as a motor trader.[39] His wife, who was living in Lennox Road, Southsea, had also turned to the courts in October 1935 to obtain an order for £2 per week maintenance.[40]

His final brush with the law was when he was arrested in London, in August 1936, for maintenance arrears, and Sybil was also suing for divorce at this point. The magistrate ordered him to be remanded in custody until the arears were paid, so it appears that possibly even his father had run out of patience with him by then. This state of affairs may well have been his motivation for going to Spain, as he left Victoria Station on 31 August 1936 along with three other pilots.[41] According to Bridgeman he had a lucrative contract for £220 per month, and an insurance which would pay his wife £2,500 in the event of his death. After signing the contract in Madrid he was admitted to the aerodrome at Getafe on 3 September 1936.

On 26 September 1936 he was flying a Nieuport Ni-D52 escorting bombers on a raid on the Toledo front. According to another British pilot this was the first time he had flown a Nieuport, having previously been confined to the Breguet Br19 bombers.[42] They were jumped by a flight of fascist Fiat or Heinkel fighters, and two were soon on Claude's tail shooting him down from 8,000 feet.

Fellow pilot Edward Hillman said on his return to the UK that Claude had 'crashed inside our lines and we were able to give him a full military funeral'.[43] His wife, Sybil said the she 'was not surprised. It was taking a big risk but Claude was like that . . . I hope he died painlessly'.[44] His long suffering father died in Bournemouth just eight weeks later.

Percy Stephen Papps (1895-1944)

Percy Stephen Papps
Courtesy of the Royal Aero Club Trust

Percy Papps was born in Portsmouth on 23 December 1895. His father manufactured pianos, and by the time he was fifteen Percy had left school and was working as a piano repairer. He joined the Royal Hampshire Regiment, and his service included a spell on the North West Frontier. By the time he was discharged he had reached the rank of Sergeant.

After marrying Dorothy in 1922, he lived at 'Valetta' in Southwood Road, on Hayling Island, near Portsmouth. He went on to open two shops, one in Chichester Road, North End, Portsmouth, and the other in Stoke Road, Gosport, where he traded as a 'Radio & Piano Specialist'.

The early 1930s also saw him gain several flying certificates. Although these certificates certainly did not qualify him to fight in the air war over Spain, he duly arrived in Los Alcazares in December 1936, no doubt attracted by the £180 per month the Spanish Republican Government was offering to pilots.[45] His efforts to go to Spain had come to the attention of the security services who had intercepted his letter to the 'Editor of the Daily Worker offering his services as pilot in Spain.' This clearly prompted further enquiries, as another note on the file reads, 'Portsmouth City Police report states that Papps is a prominent member of Portsmouth Aero Club. He is not known to associate with Communists.'[46]

An initial assessment of his flying ability included an attempt at formation flying. Ace American pilot Frank Tinker wrote that 'he was sadly lacking in experience. At one time he nearly ran into the leader's plane and disrupted the entire formation.'[47] Then after a hairy, and abortive, bombing mission, where their fighter escort went missing, Tinker noted that on their return, 'Papps, evidently a little rattled, tried to land downwind, almost ran into a Nieuport coming in from the opposite direction, and crashed. The plane did a complete cartwheel, bombs and all, but fortunately none of them exploded'.

Subsequently, Percy was largely confined to a coastal defence squadron on the eastern seaboard of Spain, undertaking reconnaissance missions and an occasional bombing mission over Teruel, but not without further mishaps.

However, that did not stop him spinning a good story when he returned home at the end of January 1937. In a briefing sent to the Admiralty, which was then passed to the Foreign Office Minister, he complained bitterly about not having been paid, and explaining how 'owing to the shocking condition of the airframes—I had three forced landings in January'. However, he also added that he 'liked the life . . . and would have done two months more if £s had been forthcoming'.[48]

His briefing was largely repeated, with a more sensationalist twist in his local paper under the headline, 'Murders and Executions Kill More Than War in Spain'. under the nom de plume of 'Cavalier'. It was a tale recounted by someone who was clearly, and luckily, removed from the main action, claiming 'there was little real fighting in the air', and also happy to recount blatantly untrue rumours of mass killings such as '70,000 are reported to have been killed in Madrid alone'.[49]

Percy briefly returned to the family business before signing up for World War Two in 1939, and leaving his wife behind in order to serve as an air traffic controller in Exeter, Devon. By 1944 he was living in Suffolk Road, Bournemouth, but working as the Control Officer at Belfast Harbour Airport. In 1944 he received the tragic news that his only child, Officer Cadet John Papps, died on active service in India, aged 18, possibly from polio. Just five weeks later on 26 November 1944, Percy himself died unexpectedly in Belfast Royal Victoria Hospital.[50]

Arthur Russell Brown (1892-1957)

Arthur Russell Browne was born on 17 November 1892, in Collingwood, Ontario, Canada. After leaving school he worked as a commercial traveller selling door to door before joining the Canadian Overseas Expeditionary Force in May 1915, serving with the 6th Canadian Field Ambulance. Two years later he was granted a transfer to the Royal Flying Corps in England, and about this time seems to have added an 'e' to his surname, along with an occasional hyphen. Just five months later, on 1 October 1917, and now a 2nd Lieutenant, he was wounded flying over the Western Front.

He was demobbed on returning to Canada in March 1919.[51] In 1926 he came back to England, and in September 1928 he married Helen Andrews in Bournemouth.[52] Their daughter Rosemary was born in 1932. At the time of going to Spain, he was working as a car salesman, and the family were living in Panorama Road, Sandbanks, Bournemouth. Having a young family the prospect of earning good money in Spain was clearly too tempting to resist, and he arrived in December 1936.

Like Percy Papps, Arthur was probably confined to coastal reconnaissance, however the experience was clearly not to his liking, possibly because payments were slow in being made. By mid-January he was back in England where he wrote an ingratiating letter to Foreign Office Minister Anthony Eden.[53] He was at pains to point out that he 'was not recruited by the Communist Party but by an agent of the Spanish Embassy.' He then explained his grievance at not being paid and said that the efforts of the Spanish Government should be 'exposed . . . as they are repudiating their payments according to the agreements.'

With his family then living in Parkstone, Poole, he returned to selling cars before re-enlisting in the RAF as a Pilot Officer in September 1939, where he was known as 'Buster' Browne. He rose through the ranks before a final promotion to Squadron Leader, in Administration and Special Duties, in January 1944.[54] After being demobbed in August 1945 he obtained a job in the Army of Occupation in Germany, as a Senior Manager in charge of transport with the Naafi.[55] This ended after he was convicted of a serious case of drink driving, in November 1952, and lost his driving licence.[56] He died in Plymouth in 1956.

Chapter Three

The formation of the British Battalion —and Jarama

The International Brigades were largely organised around nationalities and language. Initially there were only enough British volunteers to form one company, which saw action at Lopera on the Cordoba front at the end of December. However, the ranks of the British were soon numerous enough to enable the formation of a British Battalion, and at the end of January 1937 it formed part of the XV International Brigade.

Just a few weeks later, on 12 February 1937, they were thrown into battle to stop the fascists cutting the vital highway between Madrid and Valencia, at Jarama. By the end of the third day of fighting over half of the British Battalion were either dead, wounded, or taken prisoner, but the line held. Apart from two short rest periods the Battalion was to remain in the line at Jarama until 17 June, where they continued to take casualties.[57]

George William Palmer (1899-1937)

George Palmer was an ideal recruit for the International Brigades—he had spent most of his adult life in the British Army. Born on 14 March 1899 in Ealing, London, he worked as a baker's assistant before being conscripted into the Wiltshire Regiment on 4 August 1916, shortly after the death of his railway labourer father.

He was soon transferred to the Somerset Light Infantry

and posted to the Western Front in France. There he suffered gassing and trench foot but survived the war, and was discharged on 14 February 1919. Undeterred, he promptly re-enlisted in the Wiltshire Regiment the very next day and saw service in Hong Kong and India. He was discharged again due to a 'Reduction of Establishment' on 11 February 1923.

George managed to find work as a 'carman' until re-enlisting into the Army Medical Corps on 7 June 1923, seeing service in Germany and Egypt after qualifying as a medical orderly. Transferred to the Army Reserve on 6 March 1931, he was finally 'Discharged on Termination of Engagement' on 6 June 1935. He left with a ringing endorsement from his Commanding Officer, 'A good orderly who does his work well . . . Well conducted . . . He should do well in civilian life.'

Sadly, those were tough times economically and it appears that George then drifted around in search of work. He stayed with his mother, Eunice O'Brien, and her second husband, at 49 Knights Enham, in the market town of Andover, in Hampshire, between 1932 and 1933, but by December 1936 was living in a Salvation Army Hostel in London and it was from here that we went to fight in Spain.

He fought at and survived the Battle of Lopera, between 27 & 29 December 1936, where the International Brigades suffered massive losses including British poets and intellectuals John Cornford and Ralph Fox. He was then transferred to Las Rozas on the Madrid front as a Section Leader in No 1 Company of the XIV International Brigade.

It was there on 12 January 1937 that a trench he was taking cover in took a direct hit from a shell, and he was killed with 'shrapnel in the brain and heart' along with two other comrades. A British comrade, Phil Harker, with whom he had travelled from London described how George 'died trying to improve the position of his men. He died an anti-fascist soldier who had won a name for himself.'[58]

Archibald Campbell Williams (1904-1972)

Archibald Williams (known as "AC") was born in Percy Road, Southsea, Portsmouth, on 3 October 1904. Both his parents were Scottish, his shipwright father having moved the family south to the naval dockyard for work.[59] AC was the eldest of seven children and after the birth of his next four siblings, the family moved back home to Scotland. AC proved to be a very bright pupil, graduating from Invergordon Academy, where he had won a scholarship, and then finding work as an insurance clerk.

The economic depression hit the family hard, and they took the tough decision to gather what money they could to allow AC to migrate to Canada in 1923, and take up a secure job as a bank clerk in Brantford, Ontario. All was well for a while, and he was able to send some money home to support the family, but a poor decision taken on the spur of the moment was to change his life forever.

Three years after starting the job, a fire broke out in the bank. He rescued a colleague who had been overcome by the smoke and then went back in to retrieve the cash that had been left out. When he went back in a third time he found $500 which had been overlooked. This was akin to a year's salary and, unfortunately, AC gave in to a moment's temptation and put the money in his pocket. He duly ended up in front of a judge who did not consider saving a life any sort of mitigation, and was jailed for one to two years. He lost his job, home, and was disowned by his parents whom he never saw again.

On his release, AC somehow managed to avoid deportation and travelled around North America doing a variety of jobs including rancher, fur trapper, and lumberjack. However, the onset of the Great Depression made it increasingly difficult to find any sort of a job and he was forced into one of the notorious Unemployed Relief Camps. His camp was just outside Saskatoon, in the Province of Saskatchewan, which was overcrowded and the conditions appalling. Whether he had been politicised during his travels, or inside the camp, AC soon found himself as the one of the leaders of the Relief Camp delegations seeking to improve conditions. Wishing to quell any rebellion, the camp authorities decided to move the agitators to another camp in Regina, under the guise of reducing the overcrowding. The move was met with organised resistance and the police were called, resulting in something akin to a riot in which a Police Chief was accidentally killed.

As a result, twenty-six of AC's comrades stood trial for rioting, and reporters wrote that they trooped from the furniture van, which had been commandeered for use as a police wagon, into the local courthouse, singing 'The Red Flag'.[60] AC somehow managed to slip away and go on the run and it took the police another year to catch up with him. On the final day of his trial he was allowed to make his own closing address and the local newspaper records that 'He spoke for fifty-five minutes without interruption with the calm and restraint of a seasoned counsel.'[61] However, despite his eloquence the inevitable verdict of guilty was delivered, and he received two years in prison.

At the end of this prison term there was to be no escape from deportation, and on 15 December 1935 he disembarked from the SS Montclare after she had docked in Liverpool, England. Then came a long fruitless trek around the country in search of work. However, one happy outcome of his travels was a chance meeting in 1936 with a girl called Jane Orme in a London soup kitchen which led to a very happy 40 year marriage. A lack of work was compounded by the couple's concern about the rise of fascism in the UK and throughout Europe and then, of course, came the coup d'etat in Spain. By December 1936 it was decided that AC would go to fight in Spain, leaving his wife, who was by now five months pregnant, staying with friends in Portsmouth.

During this time he was also being closely observed by the British security services, having his post intercepted and phone tapped, being described as a 'Rabid agitator'.[62] Special Branch noted that AC was one of a group of sixteen who left the UK on 21 December 1936, bound for France and then down to Spain.[63] Another in the group was Alexander Foote who had been in the Fleet Air Arm in Gosport. According to Special Branch he deserted from the FAA when his attestation papers were found to be invalid, and then decided to go to Spain. He was not a member of the Communist Party so AC, whom he had befriended in Portsmouth, took him to the King Street Headquarters of the CP in London, and vouched for him.[64] [65]

After initially reporting for duty at Figueras, and then receiving basic training at Madrigueras, AC joined the No 2 Machine Gun Company. On 6 February 1937, as part of the newly formed 15th International Brigade, they were moved up to the front to enjoin in the Battle of Jarama. The British Battalion was decimated in the first two days of action with the remnants of the Machine Gun Company, including AC, being taken prisoner. They had been tricked into believing that oncoming troops, singing the 'Internationale' were from their own side, when they were, in fact, Franco's fascists.[66]

After several summary executions AC and his comrades were taken away for a brutal period of imprisonment in Talavera. It involved forced labour repairing roads and burying Republican comrades who were being executed on a nightly basis. AC's imprisonment lasted from February to April 1937, during which time his daughter was born in Portsmouth. The British prisoners were then transferred to a prison in Salamanca, where they were interrogated by a fascist officer who had been educated at Cambridge University. Judging by the transcript of AC's interrogation it is highly unlikely his interrogator discovered anything of importance that he did not already know, especially as AC would have been well aware of the possibility of being executed if he did not sound plausible.[67] AC also managed to keep a notebook whilst in Talavera and he included a detailed report of a baseball game the prisoners had organised to maintain morale, along with a list comrades who were suffering a variety of medical complaints due to their brutal treatment and poor diet.

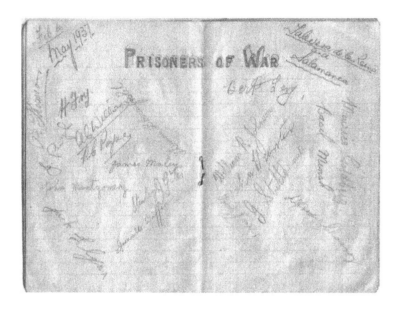

AC's notebook – Courtesy of Rosemary Williams

At the end of May 1937 most of the British prisoners, including AC, were repatriated in exchange for a group of Italian soldiers who had been taken prisoner in the battle of Guadalajara. Despite this being concrete evidence of the active involvement of the Italian Government in the war, the 'Great Democracies' of Britain, France, and America, continued to pretend that the Non Intervention Treaty was still holding. The prisoners were forced to sign a paper before leaving Spain agreeing never to return, on pain of death.

Despite this, five of them did dare to return and one of them, Jimmy Rutherford, was taken prisoner again and unlucky enough to be recognised by the interrogator from his first imprisonment, and summarily executed.

Whilst recovering from his ordeal and enjoying his family in Portsmouth, AC once again began the search for work. After an attempt to secure a job at the naval dockyard he instead took on the job of managing the Portsmouth Left Book Club Shop, in Sultan Road, Portsmouth, literally living over the shop. He and Jane also took in two of the Basque children refugees who had arrived in Southampton in 1937. The shop was subject to at least one raid by the security services, and one result of this was that an autobiographical manuscript, titled *Between Two Prison Gates*, which detailed AC's adventures in North America and Spain, and the manuscript of a play written by Jane Orme, disappeared. Disheartened, they never reproduced these texts.[68]

In May 1939, along with close friend and fellow British Brigader and prisoner, Charlie West, AC obtained employment at Wellworthy Piston Rings Ltd in Lymington. Whether they went there just for a job, or to organise the workforce, or a combination of both, is unclear. However, a note on Charlie's Special Branch file, dated November 1939 reads, 'Packer . . . Instigated unofficial strike'.[69]

It is likely that the Molotov-Ribbentrop Pact, which created a non-aggression pact between German and Russia, led to AC along with many other CP members leaving the Party. A note on one Special Branch file, dated April 1940, reads, 'CP Portsmouth believed Archie Williams had severed all connections with the CP. No further record of Archie Williams.'[70]

In 1940, in a remarkable volte-face by the British Security Forces, AC was interviewed and offered a job as a Personnel Officer at a Royal Ordnance factory, which meant moving the family to Leyland in Lancashire. His wife Jane continued to actively campaign on many important social causes, such as decent rehousing for flood victims on the east coast of England, and the resettlement of refugees created by the Suez crisis. She was also heavily involved in the Aid Spain movement and visited interned Republican soldiers at a camp in Chorley to publicise their plight.

AC worked in several factories, the final one being in Bishopton, Renfrewshire, which provided the perfect location for them to live after his retirement, not least because he was always intensely proud of his Scottish roots. It was the 'magical home' to entertain a growing family, with AC and Jane enjoying visits from their grandchildren. He also adopted his mother's family name of McAskill as one of his first names.

Sadly, AC was only able to enjoy his retirement for two years. He died on 26 June 1972 from a heart attack, after chasing deer hunters in nearby woods.

AC Williams arriving home - Daily Herald 31 May 1937

Charles James Simmons (1901?-1937)

Sadly, little is known about Charlie Simmons. His probable parents, both born in Portsmouth, were soldier Benjamin Augustus and partner Catherine. Charlie was born around 1901. At the time of the 1911 census Benjamin was stationed in the Hampshire military town of Aldershot, and from 1917 until 1939 they all lived at 5 Berkeley Street, Southsea, Portsmouth.

After a period in the British Army Charlie sought work as a painter, and was a member of the National Painters Society as well as the Communist Party.[71] He was also 'well known locally as the Literature Secretary of the National Unemployed Workers Movement in Portsmouth and a constant and hard worker for the cause of the unemployed.'[72] [73]

Charlie arrived in Spain on 7 January 1937 and was placed in No 4 Company of the British XVI Battalion.[74] He was killed on 27 February 1937 at Arganda Ridge on the Madrid-Valencia road, during the battle of Jarama.

John Kelly (1911-1979)

'Jack' Kelly was born in Liverpool on 12 February 1911, his father being a ship's steward.[75] Jack followed his father into the merchant navy and met his future wife on a call into Southampton.[76] He became a self-taught tailor who managed to talk his way into obtaining work locally, but he eventually had to travel to London to find employment. It was there that he married, giving his profession as a 'tailor's presser', and also joined the Communist Party and the United Ladies Tailoring Union.[77] Prior to leaving for Spain the couple had relocated back to Southampton, to 258 Millbrook Road.

Jack arrived in Spain on 23 December 1936 and enlisted

into the newly formed British Battalion, which was soon in action at the battle of Jarama in March/April 1937. In July 1937 a note was sent to the Communist Party headquarters in London asking for 'a responsible comrade to contact his wife and to see she gets whatever additional aid is required.'[78] By now Jack knew his wife was expecting a child, and had requested repatriation. This had been refused, no doubt because the horrendous losses at Jarama meant the Commanders felt they could spare nobody to go home. However, it appears that Jack simply deserted, and arrived home just a couple of days after his wife had given birth to twins in late August 1937.

His family were evacuated to Lyme Regis during the war, but Jack stayed in Southampton building Spitfires for Cunliffe Owen. After the war he ran his own tailoring business from home, but when work dried up he re-joined the Merchant Navy in 1947, and worked on various ships until retirement. Jack died in Southampton on 28 June 1979.

Not all the early arrivals were combatants, they also included journalists, medical staff, and volunteers for other roles such as that filled by David Gascoyne.

Jack Kelly – Courtesy of Kim Bloomfield

David Emery Gascoyne (1916-2001)

David Gascoyne was born on 10 October 1916 in Harrow, Middlesex. His bank clerk father was soon promoted to be manager of the Midland Bank in the New Forest town of Fordingbridge, Hampshire, leading to David being educated at Salisbury Choir School.[79] [80] He then attended Regents Park Polytechnic, in London, but left after failing his exams in 1932.

He then began a prolific period, building a formidable reputation as a surrealist poet, novelist, essayist and reviewer.[81] He joined the Communist Party on 21 September 1936, having come to the conclusion that 'there is no longer any honest alternative for me than direct action in the direction of Communism.'[82] Over the next four weeks he was present at demonstrations against Mosley and his Fascist Party in London, and also attended a party at the house of Esmond Romilly, who was later to fight with Ray Cox at Boadilla. David then left for Spain via Newhaven and Paris, before finally arriving in Barcelona.

He quickly made contact with the Catalonian Propaganda Ministry, and took on a job translating news bulletins during the day and broadcasting them in English every evening, largely via loudspeakers attached to lamp-posts.[83] After a short period David returned to Britain to deliver a collection of Civil War posters that were needed for a fundraising exhibition in London. He stopped off in Paris for a brief meeting with Picasso, delivering news of the artist's mother and sister in Barcelona.[84]

David returned to his writing but was plagued by mental illness, exacerbated by an addiction to amphetamines, resulting in several lengthy stays in mental hospitals. It was during a stay in Whitecroft Hospital on the Isle of Wight, where he had moved in the early 1960s to be with his parents, that he met his future wife Judy Lewis. She visited the hospital to read poetry to the patients, one of the poems being 'September Sun' which led David to introducing himself as the author. They were married in 1975, after which David found a new energy for his work, also becoming a committee member of the World Poetry Society. David died in St Mary's Hospital on the Isle of Wight on 25 November 2001.

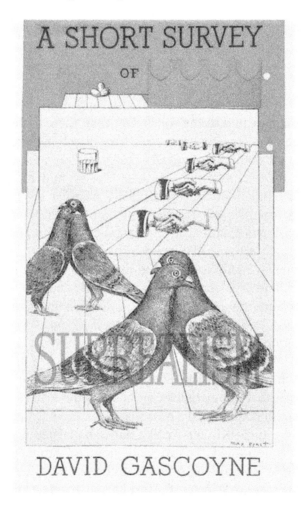

Cover of David Gascoyne's classic Survey of Surrealism, 1935

Chapter Four

The Children—and the Arrival of the SS Habana

The major casualties in any war, and those who tend to receive the least publicity, are the non-combatants. In particular children who, by virtue of their age, could not possibly have played any part in starting the conflict in which they found themselves embroiled. The Spanish Civil War was particularly traumatic for children as it was the first war in which indiscriminate bombing was used as a deliberate weapon to terrorise civilians into submission. The tactic was heartily endorsed by Franco's ally, Hitler, who saw Spain as a good arena to practice the tactics his Condor Legion would later use in the skies over Southampton, Portsmouth, and other British cities.

Efforts to ease the plight of the Spanish children, despite the indifference and shameful obstructive behaviour of the British government of the time led to two incredible initiatives which still resonate today.

The Basque Children

The most well-known episode was that of the evacuation of the Basque children to Southampton on the SS Habana.[85] By early 1937 the Basque Region had been cut off from the rest of Republican Spain, and was in imminent danger of being overrun by Franco's forces. It was also suffering constant and indiscriminate bombing from German and Italian aircraft—the deliberate bombing of Guernica on 27 April 1937, a market day, being the most famous example.

The idea of evacuating children from the war zones had been discussed by the National Joint Committee for Spanish Relief (NJCSR) since the end of 1936, and the bombing of Guernica gave an immediate urgency to the plan. In all, some 20,000 children were to be evacuated, with France taking the largest number along with Belgium, Mexico and the Soviet Union. Britain was to receive 4,000, but it was not until 18 May that the British Government finally agreed to the plan, their greater concern being that it would not be seen by Hitler and Mussolini as a breach of the phoney Non-Intervention Treaty.[86]

As part of the agreement the Government imposed stringent conditions, meaning the NJC had to guarantee that expenses for the journey and the children's upkeep while they were in Britain, all came via public donations, and that not a penny would come from the Treasury.[87] Thankfully, the evacuation received overwhelming public support, although it was not without its critics, such as Ethel Jameson, a resident of Stockbridge, Hampshire, who wrote complaining to her local paper, using the age old phrase that we 'should realise that charity begins at home'.[88]

Two doctors, Richard Ellis and Audrey Russell, were flown to Bilbao to examine the children who had been selected for the journey, and accompany them beck to Britain.[89] Ellis recounted the difficulties of examining the children around air raids, and the danger the children were facing.[90] A visit to the Civil Hospital showed that 'it was bankrupt of equipment, dressings and drugs . . . no anaesthetics to be had . . . a little boy of five was brought in . . . with eight machine-gun rounds in his belly. He died a few minutes later.'

A week before they arrived the National Joint Committee for Spanish Relief called a meeting in the Civic Centre in Southampton, to which 200 people attended to offer their help.[91] Hours before the SS Habana docked, another meeting was held in Southampton Guildhall which 1,000 people attended. A collection raised £157 and many other offers of assistance.[92]

The Habana, an old liner, finally left Bilbao harbour on 21 May 1937, loaded with 3,826 children, 95 teachers, 120 young women escorts and 15 priests. After withstanding a storm in the Bay of Biscay they arrived in Southampton early the next evening, the largest number of refugees ever to arrive in England in one day. They were taken to stay on three fields in North Stoneham, on the outskirts of the City, loaned to the local Basque Children's Committee by local Farmer George Brown of Swaythling Farm.[93] In just one week the site had been transformed by local people into a large tented camp.

It was a triumph of community organisation, which included the Co-Operative Society, led by Jack Pavey, Scouts, Guides, University students, mothers from Eastleigh. They were joined by stevedores from Southampton docks who had been organised to dig the latrines by their Communist Transport and General Workers Union shop steward, Trevor Stallard. All combined to ensure the children were made as welcome as possible. This feat was made all the more remarkable because they were originally expecting only 2,000 children, until just a few days before they actually arrived.

North Stoneham was only ever to be a brief transit camp, and the children were gradually moved out in groups to accommodation supplied by the Salvation Army, Catholic Church and more than seventy local colonies, or hostels, across the UK. The colonies included four in and around Southampton, at Rownhams Mount, Nazareth House, Southampton Training College, and Moorhill House in West End. All the colonies were sustained by the work of community groups and committees in the communities in which they were situated.

During the next few years the majority of children returned to Spain, but around 470 did stay and make their homes in

Britain. A number signed up when they were old enough to continue the war against fascism, serving in the Merchant Navy in particular. It was described by Jim Fyrth as, 'an epic of the British people's history.'[94]

Foster Parents Plan for War Children

The second initiative may not have resonated as much at the time, or indeed have received the immense credit it is due now, but the original Foster Parents Plan for Children in Spain eventually evolved into the charity Plan International. This remarkable organisation now works in over 45 countries to 'realise the rights of children and young people and to promote gender equality and girls' rights.'[95] The two British men responsible for starting the organisation were Eric Muggeridge and John Langdon-Davies.

John Eric Langdon-Davies (1897-1971)

John was born in South Africa on 18 March 1897. An only child he moved to England with his mother just a few years after his father died in 1901. He attended Tonbridge School, in Kent as a day boy between 1910-1915, and it was here that his talent as writer began to show.[96] A short spell in prison as a conscientious objector to the First World War, and marrying in 1918, thereby losing his single status, resulted in losing two scholarships, forcing him to abandon a university career in Oxford. His wife, Constance, was the daughter of an eminent doctor who lived in East Oakley House, Basingstoke. She was also a cousin of Humfrey Gilbert Scott, a British Brigader from the New Forest, who was killed at Chimorra in April 1937.

John embarked on a prestigious career, and was described by Tom Buchanan as 'a political and social activist, as an accomplished war correspondent, and student of unconventional warfare, and a brilliant populariser of science and technology'.[97] His writing took him around Britain, including Southampton where his son, Robin, was born in 1920. He also undertook lecture tours in the United States, but a spell living in Catalonia began his lifelong love affair with the Spanish region.

The first entry on his Special Branch file is as a 'Speaker at meeting in support of Spain' on 30 July 1936, less than two weeks after the fascist uprising had begun.[98] A few days later he made his second trip to Spain as a special correspondent to the left leaning 'News Chronicle.' He had ridden all the way from England on a motorbike, accompanied by his son Robin, who he then lodged with friends in Campdevanol. It is unclear if he was reassured on the question of his son's safety, writing that he was 'armed with a safe-conduct note signed by anarcho-syndicalists, one of whom in true Spanish manner told me that if anything happened to my son I should have the pleasure of shooting him.'[99]

Early in 1937 John came across a very young boy called José, one among so many orphaned or abandoned children. José had been left with a note, written by his father, which explained that his father expected to be shot when Santander fell, and pleading with whoever found his son to ensure his safety.[100] From this heart rending moment came the idea of forming colonies/hostels of children, where they would be safe and well cared for. The funds came from 'foster parents' whose monthly contributions, for individual children with whom they would correspond, provided the income to maintain the colonies. Working with the NJCSR in Britain, and in tandem with his friend, Eric Muggeridge, Foster Parents Plan for Children in Spain was developed and grown.

During the Second World War John worked as an instructor with the Home Guard, before continuing his writing as an author and reporter. He died in Shoreham, Kent, on 5 December 1971.

John Langdon-Davies (in white suit) in Catalonia, 1936.
Courtesy of Deborah Langdon-Davies

Eric George Muggeridge (1906–1988)

Eric Muggeridge was born in Sanderstead, Surrey, on 20 March 1906, the fourth of five sons. His father was a Company Secretary, who had a spell as Labour MP for Romford, along with being a long term Borough Councillor. His younger brother, Jack, recounted how Eric left school at sixteen for a job in local bank which had been arranged by his father.[101] To his father's chagrin he only lasted a year, finding it too claustrophobic. Next was a spell labouring on a smallholding, followed by working as a guide for the Workers Travel Association.[102] He also, unsuccessfully, stood for election to the local council on three successive occasions, attempting to follow in his father's footsteps.[103]

His interest in social services led to training with the Woolwich Council of Social Services, and as soon as the Spanish Civil War began he quickly volunteered as a relief worker with the NJCSR, and 'helped with the early work of evacuating Madrid and other besieged cities . . . [and assisted] in building up the Children's Colonies for youngsters who had been orphaned by the war'.[104] The security services began to take an interest in him when he made another trip to Spain on 16 January 1937, not returning to England until the 21 November 1937.[105] He then went immediately to the USA to set up a branch of the Foster Parents Plan there, spending the next year speaking to over 400 meetings and becoming its Executive Secretary.

He arrived back in the UK on 19 December 1938, but with the imminent fall of Catalonia to the fascists he was soon on his way back to Spain to help evacuate children to France. He arrived on 26 January 1939, the day Barcelona fell.[106] Amid the mayhem of floods of panicking refugees fleeing for the border, and the constant bombing and strafing by Fascist aircraft, Eric worked to get two truckloads of 50 children, and colony staff, into France and safety. Not content with this, and

43

with his life clearly in danger, Eric made further trips back into Catalonia trying to locate children and get them out. One example is highlighted in a telegram, dated 4 February 1939, sent to 'Foster Parents New York' which read, 'Extreme emergency. Now required immediate evacuation to France of every child possible. Figueras under incessant bombardment. Collected 130 children from cinema. Had been sitting in complete darkness with fear, waiting for help. Have located further foster children and arranging transfer to Biarritz.'

Eric Muggeridge – Courtesy of Jackson Towie

He was to spend the next five years shuttling between the colonies in France and Britain, and speaking engagements in the USA, his responsibilities having increased when John Langdon-Davies resigned in 1940 to serve as a war correspondent in Finland. He left PLAN after being called up in 1944. Post World War Two, Eric worked in Allied Germany during the reconstruction, then moved back to the UK in 1948 when his daughter was born.[107] For most of the 1950s and early 1960s, he worked in the Colonial Service serving as a Development Officer in Nigeria until 1966, when he returned to live in Hove, Sussex.[108]

Despite his heroism in Spain, and his continuing legacy of Plan International, the only Muggeridge most British people have heard of is his brother Malcolm (1903-1990) a journalist and satirist who was a regular feature on television for many years. This was highlighted in a newspaper article headlined 'Malcolm's Brother' which described how Eric was waiting for a job to come up, his previous one having been as a ships steward in the first class lounge of the QE2. Some of his previous exploits were recounted with his time in Spain being dismissed as simply, 'during the Spanish Civil War he ran a campaign to look after war orphans'. Eric died in Brighton in March 1988. Although he may not have received the recognition he deserved, children across the world continue to be helped as a result of his work, a truly heroic legacy.

Chapter Five

Other events in 1937—post Jarama

The British Battalion saw further action in the Brunette offensive in July, and at Quinto in the Aragon offensive at the end of August. However, Hampshire Brigaders were also involved on other battlefields in Spain.

Humfry Gilbert (Alexander) Scott (1904-1937)

Humfry Scott was born in Bournemouth, on 28 December 1904, the fifth son and ninth of ten children born to his surgeon father Bernard and mother Lydia. The family lived in 'Kettlethorns' in the village of Sway in the New Forest, and their main house Fairlea on the West Cliff in Bournemouth.

He was educated at Saugeen Prep School in Bournemouth, and then Bradfield College near Reading. His older brother, Tom, noted his total disregard for the school rules and customs that were supposed to apply during a pupil's first year. However, 'there was just something about him so that nobody ever corrected him.'[109] Humfry then won a classical scholarship to St John's College, Oxford, from where he graduated in November 1927.

After spells working at the Bodleian Library, in Oxford, and then as a teacher at Edinburgh Academy, he left for Vienna working as teacher and translator.[110] He then went on to spend six years working in Moscow and Leningrad in the Cooperative Publishing Society of Foreign Workers, as editor and translator. Unbeknown to his family until after his death, whilst in Moscow he met and married a Sudetan German, Hedwig (Hedi) Zappe. Although a 'sympathiser'[111] he never

46

joined the Communist Party, but he was the Trade Union Organiser for the British Section in the Publishing Society.

Humfrey Scott in 1936 – Courtesy of Elena Duran

From Moscow he left for Spain, arriving on 24 February 1937. He was soon elected a political delegate to the 2nd Company of the Anglo/US XX Battalion. In March 1937 the Company were moved up to the Cordoba front. Company Commissar, American, John Gates recalled, 'Exactly three weeks after we had landed in Spain, and after each of us had fired only three rounds of ammunition in training, we were in combat'.[112] Fellow No 2 Company comrade, Irishman Joe Monks, described how Alexander Scott (apparently his name in the company), 'loathed religion and nationalism, and he expressed pleasure in being a comrade of four godless

Irishmen in the XX Battalion'.[113] John Gates wrote to Hedi and described how, 'The position we occupied at the front was a very dangerous one—dominated by the enemy from a superior height and under heavy sniping fire at all times. We were daily subjected to heavy artillery and aviation bombardments at all times. In all this Scott occupied one of the front trenches. On the day of the fatal action, under cover of artillery fire the enemy (Moors) advanced to within 10 metres of our position and surprised us with hand grenades, forcing us from our position. In this, Comrade Scott, in his position, was killed by a hand grenade before he knew what had happened. He was killed instantly.'[114]

In a letter to Walter Tapsell, British Commissar at the base in Albacete, John Gates wrote, 'I am especially sorry to report the death of Humphrey (sic) Scott, political delegate of the English Section of our company, who was killed by a hand grenade during an enemy attack against our positions on 21 April. Scott was my right hand man in political work and was very valuable to us. His is a great loss'.[115]

Michael Edward John Livesay (1915-1937)

Michael Livesay was born in a nursing home in Granada Road, Southsea, Portsmouth on 10 December 1915. His father, Paymaster Commander Augustus, was a career Royal Navy Officer who had just finished a long posting on Ascension Island, where daughter Margery was born in 1911, and Australia. His mother Kate arrived back in the UK just few months before Michael's birth, and the family then lived for a short time with Augustus's parents in nearby Bury Road, Gosport.

The Livesay family were notable for their architectural and artistic achievements. Michael's Uncle George, Grandfather John, and Great Grandfather Augustus, were all noted architects, particularly of churches in southern England, but also including the Protestant Chapel in Rome. His Uncle John migrated to Canada where he built the largest publishing company in the country, Canada Press, and amongst his children was Dorothy, who became perhaps Canada's greatest ever progressive poet. John also helped form the Progressive Arts Club whose later members included Mac-Pap Brigader Charlie Saunders, formerly from Portsmouth. Michael's Aunt Fanny was a noted artist and lived in a family home, Sandrock Spring in Chale, on the Isle of Wight, which was often used as a base when the extended Livesay family were in the UK.

Following the great family tradition Michael enrolled at the Architectural Association (AA), in London, in 1933, for a four year course to become an accredited architect. Despite achieving good marks throughout he was forced to leave at the end of his second year.[116] The AA records merely state that the first two instalments of that year were paid on time, and the third missed, a pencil note stating 'father abroad paying later'.[117] However, the local paper goes into more detail of a drastic change in family circumstances, reporting that Augustus was convicted at Winchester Assizes for 'attempting to procure another person for an improper purpose' and sentenced to six months' imprisonment.[118] In a further cruel twist, his Military Service record noted that 'he is to be removed from the Retired List in consequence of a conviction by the Civil Power on 6 July 1933'.[119] Removal from the Retired List would have meant the loss of his service pension.

After his release Augustus travelled to South Africa as a merchant, in November 1934, and was reported as having died there on 19 June 1935.

It is almost certain that Michael was politicised at the AA which had a strong left wing grouping at that time. He joined the Association of Architects, Surveyors, and Technical Assistants, and the CPGB.[120] His address was given as 26 Brunswick Square, London, on leaving for Spain, where he arrived on 21 January 1937 to join the British Battalion of the International Brigades.

After surviving the Battle of Jarama, Michael was utilised as a cartographer in a scout unit attached to the British Battalion's Brigade staff.[121] Fellow Brigader Jason Gurney records how Michael's language skills in French and German got him transferred to the XIV Battalion as Battalion Commander George Nathan's interpreter.[122] It is possible that Michael met the famous author Stephen Spender during this time. Spender describes how he met M___ who suggested that he had found the 'Brigade was run by Communists, for whom he had no sympathy' and claimed that M___ had added, 'My life is to walk up to the ridge here every day until I am killed'.[123] It is difficult to know if Michael had become disillusioned or whether Spender was simply using him to voice his own unhappiness at the Communist Party. However, as Michael was an active member of the Party before Spain, their influence would have been no surprise to him.

Michael Livesay
Courtesy of University of Manitoba Archives & Special Collections
(Dorothy Livesay Collection)

Whatever his thoughts may have been, Michael continued to do his duty bravely until he was mortally wounded, probably by artillery fire, at La Segovia, and died of his wounds on 2 June 1937.

His death was poignantly recorded by a young British nurse, Thora Silverthorne, who wrote, 'We had become close friends during our rest periods. He was brought into the hospital badly wounded but was conscious and was so relieved to be brought into the theatre where Broggi and I were working.[124] We chatted and I held his hand whilst he was having the anaesthetic—he did not recover consciousness. I collected Michael's passport and odd articles and sent them to his mother when I returned to England. I never met her but wrote to her about his work, our friendship and his death. He died quite peacefully—indeed we were far more shaken than he. His character was the greater for he hated war, he hated the dirt the bad food—he was in no way intoxicated emotionally—he was just following his plain duty and placing his ability and his service at the disposal of something greater than the individual—the future of humanity. He died more surely for his country than those in 1914-1918, for this war concerns ALL of us . . . We cannot forget Michael, nor can we forget those other faces we shall see no more in the Brigade'.[125]

With Aunt Fanny having died in 1931, Michael's mother Kate, gave instructions for Sandrock Spring to be auctioned in June 1938 and she died in a nursing home in Hindhead, Surry, in 1950. Michael's sister Margery, a stenographer, had married earlier in 1950, and died childless in 1978. Even the beautiful Sandrock Spring failed to survive, having been lost in one of the Isle of Wight's frequent landslips some years ago.

Aubrey Redman aka William Harvey
(1919-1981)

Aubrey Redman was born in Portsmouth on 10 March 1919 the third of six children to labourer William and his wife Ada. After school he joined the British Army but soon deserted, leaving home at Prince George Street in Portsmouth, and going on the run from the military police to east London.[126]

He adopted the name of his elder brother, and his year of birth (1916), taking the alias of William Harvey, which he was to retain for the rest of his life.

He arrived in Spain on 4 January 1937, and was soon in action on the Jarama front from 12 February, being wounded on the 27 February in the left hand and losing the top of one of his fingers.[127] [128] He was in hospital for six weeks but then returned to the front, where he deserted on the first day of the battle of Brunette on 6 July 1937.[129] He seems to have spent the rest of his time in Spain on the run or in prison. On one occasion he was arrested with three other British deserters by the Valencia port police, in the hold of a British ship.[130]

Ironically, had he been honest about his age he would never have been in such a position, as the International Brigades tried to prevent anyone under the age of 21 from enlisting. In the meantime, his frantic mother wrote to Brigade Headquarters pointing out that he was only 18 years old, and asking where he was.[131] She added that she had received a response from the British Communist Party saying he was in the training camp in Albacete. A year earlier she had lobbied the Foreign Office, but as a letter from the British Consulate in Valencia to the Consul General in Barcelona makes clear, 'there is nothing which can be done beyond noting the man's name in case he turns up as a deserter or otherwise'.[132]

Aubrey finally arrived back home in late 1938 and it is

believed that he re-enlisted in the British Army, still under the name of Harvey, during the Second World War. He later worked as a night security guard at a Portsmouth paint factory before passing away in July 1981.

Henry Abbott (1896-1939)

Harry Abbott was one of the first, and oldest, recruits to the International Brigades. Born in Blackburn on 27 June 1896, he began working life as a weaver before becoming a nurse attendant at a local mental health colony. There he met nurse Annie Foley and they married in 1923, having three children before moving to new jobs at the Coldeast Colony, near Fareham in Hampshire.

Politically active in the National Association for Local Government Officers (NALGO) and the Communist Party, it was from there that he left to join the fight in Spain at the end of December 1936. Sadly, Harry's war in Spain was over almost as soon as he arrived at the training base in Madrigueras, when he broke his ankle.[133] During the time it took to heal, he did little more than guard duty at the base, and by June 1937 it was decided that on the grounds of age and demoralisation he should be repatriated. He arrived back in the UK on 13 July 1937.[134]

Sadly for Harry, his life took a further turn for the worse. In 1939 he was of 'no fixed abode' living in a common lodging house in Redruth, Cornwall, whilst working as a porter.[135] He had told of being a weaver and coming from Lancashire, seemingly avoiding memories of his family who were still in the Coldeast Colony. On 19 September 1939 he decided, once again, to fight fascism and took an army medical which found him fit for 'home service'.[136] He then reported to the local drill hall in Truro where he enlisted in the Duke of Cornwall's Light Infantry. Within minutes fate then played another cruel, and final, trick on Harry when he was struck down with a massive fatal heart attack.[137] When asked by the Coroner at the inquest as to whether he was doing anything to cause him to collapse, the witness replied that he was simply changing into Army clothing and speculated that maybe 'the excitement of renewing acquaintance with khaki proved too much for him'.[138]

Whilst both his attempts to take up arms against fascism were thwarted, at least Harry's last attempt is permanently recognised, as his few minutes of enlistment means he is recorded on the Roll of Honour of those who lost their lives in World War Two.

The overwhelming majority of international volunteers joined the International Brigades, which were incorporated into the command structure of the Spanish Republican Army. However, a number joined one of the numerous militias which formed in reaction to the start of the coup and resisted any formal integration. Among these were the large Anarchist movement and POUM, which volunteers from the Independent Labour Party decided to join.[139] [140]

Stafford Leslie Charles Cottman (1918-1999)

Staff Cottman was born in a nice house alongside Peartree Green in east Southampton on 6 March 1918. His father was an officer in the Merchant Navy, eventually becoming Captain of the only Russian oil tanker in the UK, before being killed in a traffic accident on Preston Docks in October 1935.[141] Owing to his father's job the family moved around the country, and Staff was largely educated in London and Bristol. He was also sent to Socialist Sunday School at the age of eleven, and joined the Young Communist League when he was about seventeen years old.[142]

Staff decided to go to Spain, saying later that he 'felt a

personal disgust that Franco should get military aid from Hitler and Mussolini, whilst Britain and France agreed on a non-intervention policy, which starved the rightful Government of Spain of arms and meant Spanish workers bled to death. Surely it must be wrong to do nothing. So I volunteered to fight for the Spanish people on the side of the elected Government'.[143] He applied to both the Communist Party and the Independent Labour Party (ILP). The ILP replied first, and so Staff became the youngest member of their contingent when they left for Spain on 10 January 1937.[144] [145] In Spain the ILP volunteers allied themselves to their sister party, the Workers' Party of Marxist Unification (POUM). Rudimentary military training took place at the Lenin Barracks in Barcelona before they were posted to the Aragon and Huesca fronts from January to March 1937.[146] Staff commented that, 'There was little action on this front except spasmodic firing into the hills opposite which were held by Fascists'.[147] It was at this time that Staff met George Orwell, who had also joined POUM, and thus began a lifelong friendship between the two of them.

In May 1937 the ILP went on leave to Barcelona.[148] Unfortunately, this coincided with a complete breakdown in the loose alliance between the Anarchists and POUM on one side and the communist supported Government on the other. Bitter fighting broke out, centred on the Anarchist held telephone exchange in the centre of Barcelona which lasted for several days before the Anarchists and POUM laid down their arms. This was followed by POUM being labelled as fascist and outlawed, with its leadership being pursued and imprisoned. Rightly fearing for his life and liberty Staff went into hiding, eventually managing to catch a train back across the border into France.

Once back in Britain, Staff was hounded by the Communist Party due to his involvement with POUM, and expelled from the Young Communist League. He left this mother in Bristol to go and work for the ILP in London, and gave active support to the 'Aid for Spain' movement. When war broke out in 1939 he registered as conscientious objector, such was his continuing anger at the earlier appeasement policy of the Government, and their failure to help Spain. He argued his case at a tribunal which was chaired by the historian and academic H.A.L. Fisher,[149] whose British International Brigader nephew, Herbert, was lost in the retreats through Aragon. Like so many of the volunteers who fought in Spain he argued that World War Two would not have happened if fascism had been defeated in Spain.

A year later with France having fallen, and believing he had made his point, Staff joined Bomber Command as a rear gunner, surviving numerous missions over enemy held territory. The day before his aircraft was eventually shot down he was invalided out of flight duties with a burst ear drum. After retraining as an airfield controller he was posted to Northern Ireland where he met his wife, Stella.

After the war he worked as a clerk with the British Overseas Aircraft Corporation, and moved to Eastcote in the London Borough of Hillingdon. He remained active in local politics, standing as a Labour Party candidate for Hillingdon Council. Staff remained a socialist all his life, believing in people and justice and not possessions, often telling his wife, 'I only need one shirt because I can only wear one.'[150] Staff died in Bath on 19 September 1999.[151]

Chapter Six

January/February 1938—The Battle of Teruel

In early January 1938, in dreadful freezing conditions, Spanish Republican Troops captured the town of Teruel. Within days, the Fascists counter attacked and the International Brigades were sent to reinforce the position and try and hold the town. The terrible winter conditions which caused more casualties than enemy fire, along with the enemy's superior numbers and heavy artillery forced a withdrawal at the end of February.

Arthur Gordon Robey Blackman (1915-2004)

Arthur Blackman was born on the 20 January 1915 in the long disappeared Carnarvon Arms pub in Newbury, the son of publican Ernest and his wife Alice. At the time of leaving for Spain in May 1937, Arthur was living in Hammersmith, London, working as a hairdresser, and had joined the Communist Party. The contact address he gave was 92 Stuart Crescent, in Stanmore, Winchester, the home of his mother and two sisters.

Frank Deegan, a casual docker from Liverpool, described the arduous journey he and Arthur took, along with six others, to get to Spain.[152] In January 1937 the British Government had passed the Foreign Enlistment Act which made it illegal for British nationals to volunteer to fight in Spain. Although, ultimately, nobody was ever prosecuted under this law, the penalties were severe, so volunteers were careful to try and avoid bringing attention to themselves. Their journey began by meeting in London and then getting a weekend ticket to Paris, as passports were not necessary, at that time, for such a trip.

The next problem was the journey into Spain, as the so called 'great democracies' of Britain and America had pressured France into shutting their border with Spain. This was against the backdrop of the non-intervention treaty whereby the major countries of the world had agreed not to intervene in Spain. This effectively meant that the democratically elected government of Spain was denied the right, enshrined in international law, to buy arms and equipment on the open market. Meanwhile, Nazi Germany and fascist Italy continued to pour in men, aircraft and heavy artillery, factors which were to prove decisive in determining the outcome of the war.

After gathering in Paris the volunteers, from over fifty countries, were split into small groups who then took the train to Perpignan. From there the final part of the journey was a dangerous overnight walk over the Pyrenees, guided by local men who were usually local smugglers. After arriving at the reception point in Madrigueras it was then on to Albacete for training and deployment to an active unit.

Arthur and his group arrived in Spain on 1 June 1937. After training he was assigned to No 1 Company of the XVI (British) Battalion, XV International Brigade, and spent time at the Company Headquarters as the clerk and first aid man.[153] He was soon in trouble and, on 17 July 1937, found himself jailed for five days on a charge of being absent without leave in Albacete, although this is his only recorded indiscretion.[154] Certainly his conduct must have improved because in October 1937 he was a Sergeant in the 15th Brigade medical services.[155]

In January 1938 the Battalion were moved up the line and thrown into the bloody battle of Teruel. On 20 January No 1 Company covered the retreat of the Battalion under a heavy fascist bombardment. Eighteen British Brigaders were killed and twenty-five wounded including Arthur.[156] He spent several weeks in hospital, suffering from shell shock and with a wounded foot.[157] The foot injury was to cause him problems all his life, resulting in two further operations sometime after he returned home from Spain.[158] It was not long after leaving hospital that he was repatriated back to Britain.

The 1939 Electoral Register shows that he was living in Holborn and working as a hairdresser and ledger clerk. With the outbreak of war his injury in Spain meant he was unfit for active service, but in July 1944 he was able to sign on for the Merchant Navy, where he served until 1949.[159]

Arthur lived the rest of his life in London, marrying in January 1951 and having a son. He worked as a railway clerk, and died on 21 January 2004.

Arthur Blackman – Courtesy of Chris Blackman

Albert Edward Rabone (1916-1938)

Albert Rabone was born in the family home at 11 Woodstock Road, Gosport, on 3 July 1916, the youngest of the four children who had survived infancy. Sadly, his mother died just two years later. After attending Newtown School, and then after a year as an errand boy, he joined the Royal Navy, aged fifteen, as a 'Signalboy'.[160] Three years later he was discharged, he claimed heroically 'for having Red tendencies'.[161] Unfortunately, the truth was later disclosed in a court case where the Bench was told, 'he was of good character till he entered on man's service in the Royal Navy, when he got into bad company and deserted ship'. He was sentenced to twenty eight days detention and was discharged from the Navy'.[162]

He then spent the following year 'roaming England', which included serving three months imprisonment for robbery, and culminated with him ending up in the dock at the Hampshire Quarter Sessions in October 1936, charged with a burglary and a 'smash and grab'. Not for the last time the court leant towards leniency, as the Chairman thought he should really go to Borstal but, instead, bound him over for two years.

Probably because his life had no obvious purpose, and with the war in Spain offering some sort of excitement, Albert left for Spain in new year of 1937 arriving in the garrison base of Figueras on 5 January. What followed was possibly the most bizarre career of any of the British International Brigaders, albeit sadly ending in tragedy, and perhaps best told in chronological order.[163]

January 1937: Spent at the training base at Madrigueras, and placed in No 4 Company of the 16th Battalion.

10 February: Moved up to the Jarama front, near to the rear HQ at Morata de Tajuna. Over the next weeks the fighting was very intense with the British Battalion, including No 4 Company taking heavy losses, but they held the line.

24 March: A letter from Albert postmarked Albacete, dated 7 March, was printed in his local newspaper, 'contradicting certain articles published in various newspapers in England about the English battalion.' [164] He explained that everyone, 'enlisted on their own free will, including myself, and not one has regretted it . . . I hope that the people of Gosport and Portsmouth will think for themselves, and not listen to these stories, and get together to help the Spanish people in their fight for liberty and their rights'.

Early May: Albert was involved in a traffic accident resulting in week in hospital in Morata, before returning to the front. He complained that, 'I had now been four straight months in the line and was worn . . . and on 20 May I left the line'.[165]

28 or 29 May: He reported back to 'Comrade Robson' (in London) and went home where he gave a long interview to his local paper, which the reporter described as 'the plain, unvarnished, and possibly unromantic story of a Gosport man's experiences fighting for the International Brigade British Battalion in Spain'.[166] [167] Albert described his experiences after his arrival in Spain, in particular detailing the bloody battle of Jarama and its aftermath. Interestingly, he did not attempt to glorify his own part in this or, not unreasonably, admit he had deserted. In fact he finished the interview by saying, 'When I left to come home things were fairly quiet. Despite all we have gone through we have nothing to complain about.'

5 June: Albert decided to return to Spain. He reported back to London, leaving the same night and arriving about six days later. After a spell in Madrigueras he was sent to the Brunette front.

20 July: He wrote 'My nerves went as the result of aircraft and I left the line and made for Cartagena'.[168] He managed to get on board a ship but was arrested and imprisoned for two months, after which he was sent to Albacete.

61

October: From Albacete he went to be reunited with the British Battalion in Ambite, as a Battalion scout.

7 January 1938: A further letter from Albert is printed in the local paper, 'sending greetings to the people of Gosport and Hampshire for the coming year.' He added, 'Our glorious Brigade . . . has done excellent work. Today the spirit is marvellous and will never be broken, so it is a cert that Franco and Mussolini will be driven from Spanish soil'. [169]

14 January: The Battalion is moved up to the very front of the Republican position on the Teruel front, a battle where more men were lost to the cold than were killed in battle.[170]

25 January: Albert is wounded in the forearm and face by shrapnel. After three weeks in hospital he was declared fit and sent back to Albacete.

Early March: Along with a group of others Albert was ordered back to the front. He got as far as Reus, but while waiting for a train, 'we were bombed and it seemed to upset three of us, so we decided to go home'.

15 March: Along with Englishman John Webster, and Canadian Ross Madley, Albert made it as far as the French border before being arrested.[171]

Precisely what happened next is unknown, however two undated notes in the Battalion files record that, 'Presumably got away again as is reported as having been killed falling down hold of a ship'. The other note adds, 'Ross Madley No 3 Company Mac-Paps is authority'.[172]

William George Alexander (1910–2000)

Bill Alexander was born in the Hampshire market town of Ringwood on 13 June 1910. His mother was a village school teacher, left to bring up seven children when his carpenter father died in 1917. Despite a poverty stricken childhood Bill won a scholarship from his council infant school to a secondary school and then on to Reading University, where he graduated with an Honours Degree in chemistry in 1931.[173]

After university he started work as an industrial chemist at a paper mill in Dartford and, in 1933, became a lifelong member of the Communist Party.[174] He was also an active member of the National Union of Printing, Bookbinding & Paper Workers, serving on its Branch Committee.[175] Along with other future British Brigaders he saw action on the streets of London in the Battle of Cable Street, preventing Oswald Mosley's fascists from marching through the east end of London.[176]

Bill arrived in Spain on 22 May 1937, and after training in Tarazona he was placed in the Anti-Tank Battery of the XV Brigade, later becoming its Commissar.[177] Whilst with the Battery he was cited for bravery at Belchite in September 1937.[178] He was then transferred to the British Battalion on 12 November 1937 as its Adjutant, with the rank of Lieutenant.[179]

Just six weeks later on the Teruel front he was appointed Battalion Commander, when Fred Copeman was repatriated following complications from an operation for appendicitis.[180] His later actions in leading the Battalion, during one of the many bloody episodes of the battle of Teruel, would see him promoted in the field to Captain.[181] His active role in Spain came to an end on 17 February 1938, at Segura de los Baños, when he was badly wounded in the same action in which Harold Laws, from Southampton, was killed. After months in hospital Bill was invalided home in late June 1938.

Back home in Southwark, London he shared a house, and air raid warden duties, with fellow Brigader and printer Lou Kenton.[182] Following a recommendation from the 'Red' Duchess of Atholl, in 1940, he was granted a commission at the Sandhurst Military Academy, where he finished top of his class.[183] He saw active service in North Africa, Italy, France and Germany before being demobbed in 1946, with the rank of Captain in the Reconnaissance Corps.[184]

After the war he resumed full-time work for the Communist Party and was the Coventry secretary until 1947, standing unsuccessfully as a Communist in Coventry East in the 1945 General Election. He then spent six years as secretary of the Midlands area, and another six years as secretary for Wales, became assistant general secretary of the party in 1959, a position he held until 1967. He later taught chemistry in a comprehensive school in south-east London until retirement.[185]

The greatest legacy of Bill Alexander must surely be the organisation which keeps alive the memory of the British Brigaders and continually reminds people what took them to Spain, and the lessons we all need to heed from that period. The International Brigade Association (IBA) was formally set up on 9 March 1939, with membership confined to the men and women who had actually served in Spain. They agreed that the aim and purpose of the Association was: 'To carry on in Britain the spirit and traditions of the International Brigade as front line fighters for the defence and advance of democracy against fascism, for the rapid development of common action and purpose among all anti-fascist people by spreading the truth about the struggle of the people, Army and Government of Republican Spain and to win all necessary support for the Spanish Republic.'[186]

Bill began with the position of Vice-Chair of the IBA later becoming its Secretary until his death.[187] Although married with a family, and full time job, Bill spent much of the rest of his life fiercely defending and promoting the memory of the International Brigades. As well as addressing countless meetings, it also included being involved in authoring at least three books, and various pamphlets. From 1989-1996 he was the President of the Marx Memorial Library in Clerkenwell, London, which still holds the British Battalion archive.

Bill Alexander died on 11 July 2000. At his funeral fellow British Brigader and former General Secretary of the

Transport & General Workers Union, Jack Jones, paid his respects to 'a very great fighter for the people—a fine and decent man who contributed greatly to the welfare of others.' Jack said that no-one had done more to ensure that the traditions of the International Brigade were disseminated among the people, especially young people. 'He spread the values of internationalism, opposition to racism, the need for more equality in the world and opposition to all forms of fascist reaction.'[188]

Harold Laws (1911-1938)

Harry Laws was born on the 20 June 1911 the only son to his father, Herbert, who was the General Manager of the Southampton Co-operative Society.[189] With his sister, Margaret (Peggy), the family lived initially at 47 Bishops Road, Itchen, Southampton, later moving a short distance to 24 Stoddart Avenue in Bitterne, Southampton.[190]

After leaving Itchen Secondary School, Harry was apprenticed to a Southampton engineering company, and in 1928 he joined the Amalgamated Engineering Union. In 1933 he left Southampton and went to Peterborough, from Worcester, in 1935, to work as a turner at Baker Perkins. He held very advanced political views and, after a short time with the Labour Party he joined the Communists with whom he had been associated at Southampton. He also joined the No 5 Branch AEU and represented that body on the local Trades and Labour Council. The agent of Peterborough Labour Party said that Laws had done a great deal of work for the Party: 'Never mind his political views, he was a good boy, and he had the courage of his convictions.'[191] The paper pointed out that Harry was also a keen cyclist, and that as soon as he arrived in Peterborough he had joined the Clarion, and the Peterborough Club, taking part in their runs, going off alone, or with one or two friends.

In 1936 he moved to London, and variously lived in Walthamstow and Willesden before leaving for Spain, where he arrived on 17 October 1937. Thankfully Harry, like Herbert Fisher, was a great letter writer, and a number of letters to his sister Peggy have survived. After a month's training at Albacete he wrote, 'I enjoy firing a rifle very much and expect to enjoy it more when there's a fascist at the other end'. At the beginning of January 1938 Harry, by now promoted to Cabo (Corporal), and the rest of No 2 Company of the British Battalion were moved from reserve positions to the front line at the battle of Teruel. 'There was the fairy land of snow and glittering mountains of the Teruel when we took up reserve positions. The cruel march across snow and ice to the front line when we had to stop every fifteen minutes and rub our ungloved hands in snow to prevent frostbite. There was a nightmare trek over three kilometres of no-man's land for guns and ammunition. Now it had thawed and made the going treacherous. A glorious daybreak disclosing the fascist positions in front of a ruined building with a red, blue, gold, and white mountain at the back. Cocks crowing somewhere then the rattle of a fascist machine gun broke the peace. Pretty soon our artillery from way back starts to shell a man and mule. I wake up and execute a few lice, I think I got the ringleaders but it must be a genuine rank and file movement for they are very active.'

He continued, 'Plenty of bullets flying about, mostly fascist now. The artillery man is trying to hit another mule. I make my way back to the trench in safety and volunteer to fetch the dinner. Three kilometre walk, swell scenery. Returning with the food a fascist machine gun starts to bark at us. We make it safely and report the road under fire. More sleep with a Boom, Boom, Boom, as a lullaby.'

On 14 January Harry was wounded. Writing to a friend in Peterborough from his hospital bed he complained, 'I only fired five shots, and I can't recollect hitting anything. Franco got me. So the first round goes to Franco'.[192] Writing to Peggy he said, 'Just to let you know I am still enjoying the sunshine under the palm trees by the sea. I was on the Teruel front for eleven days and finally got a small bullet wound in the right arm which has nearly healed'.

Whilst in hospital he wrote again to Peggy, a letter which his brother-in-law Henry had printed in the Oxford Gazette. He described a bombing raid on his hospital: 'Isabela, the nurse, flitted past my bed, slapped me hard on the cheek, and cried in a startled voice, 'Avión! Camarada! Avión!' . . . Jaundice makes you feel dopey and it was some seconds before I realised that it was the Fascists coming to bomb hell out of us . . . My heart by this time was beating pretty fast and I felt again as I did when fighting the Fascists in London, when, just as we were breaking through a police cordon, the bastards turned, drew their truncheons and charged. Then, as now, I felt the pitch of excitement which in a second would turn to fear or courage . . . I heard something whistle through the air, and Wham, the room was full of flying glass, the windows caved in, and the empty beds danced about the floor. Wham! Wham! The crash of falling buildings and roofs . . . Two days later I was moved from this town. On the third the Fascists came again. Isabela, the nurse, a beautiful cultured girl Spanish girl of 20, had her right arm torn away. Such is the path of Fascism. How we long to win the war, and how determined we are to stamp Fascism out of Spain.'[193]

Tragically, Harry was subsequently killed at Segura de los Baños on 17 February 1938. Details of how this came about were disclosed to his family in a letter his mother received from Sam Wild, Commander of the British Battalion, after his death. Sam explained how 'Harold was first wounded at a place called Celadas, it was not a serious wound but sufficient to keep him out of the line for a few weeks. But Harold could not stay away whilst the remainder of the Battalion were in action so he re-joined the Battalion whilst we were in action at Teruel. His wound in the arm was still open and on one occasion I managed to get him away to get the proper treatment but he again returned.'

Sam Wild himself was wounded on four separate occasions in Spain. Such was the commitment and courage of the International Brigaders in the fight against fascism. He said that he 'knew Harold as a splendid soldier and comrade and his work was always beyond reproof.' and that, 'after the action at Teruel we moved to a place called Segura de los Baños where Harold was killed taking part in a successful advance by the British Battalion.'[194]

On hearing the news of his death his father told the local paper, 'Although I do not share his views, I know that he was filled with the zeal and idealism of youth. He was a most unselfish boy—in fact, he never thought of himself at all . . . Right up till the last he was thoroughly convinced that he was doing the right thing, and he had no regrets'.[195]

Harold Laws – Courtesy of Henrietta Quinnell & Catherine Silman

Chapter Seven

March/April 1938—The Retreats through Aragon

On 9 March 1938 the fascists launched a massive offensive in Aragon, which would see them succeed in driving all the way through to the Mediterranean and splitting the Spanish Republic in two. Every available man was thrown into the battle to try to stem the advance. Once again the British Battalion was to find itself in the front line, and taking another dreadful battering.

Herbert Douglas Fisher (1910-1938)

Herbert Fisher was born in London on 20 October 1910, into a family with an extraordinary record of public service. Amongst his uncles, HAL was a legendary Warden at New College Oxford and a Cabinet Minister in Lloyd-George's government. Charles was a much respected Oxford don and Sussex county cricketer, who insisted on enlisting despite being over age in World War One. He served in France, being mentioned in despatches, before transferring to the Navy as a Lieutenant on the battle cruiser HMS Invincible, and going down with the ship during the Battle of Jutland. Another Uncle, Admiral Sir William was Commander in Chief of the Mediterranean Fleet, and Edwin became Chairman of Barclay's Bank. Aunt Adeline, with whom Herbert corresponded whilst in Spain, was the first wife of composer Ralph Vaughan Williams.

Herbert's father, Edmund, was a much respected architect whose designs included the hall at Somerville College, Oxford, and the Holy Trinity Protestant Church in Rome. Like his brother Charles he also insisted on joining up, despite being well over age. He saw action at the Battle of Ypres before being invalided home with appendicitis, where he died on Easter Sunday 1918, when Herbert was just eight years old.

As with generations of Fishers before and since, Herbert attended the progressive Dragon Preparatory School in Oxford. He attended from 1920 until 1924 when he went on to King William's College, on the Isle of Man. On leaving there in 1929 he moved into the pottery trade. He served a three year apprenticeship as a designer with Ashtead Potters, in Surrey, whose Chairman was Sir Stafford Cripps.[196] He then moved to a pottery in Staffordshire from where he wrote to his mother in October 1935, congratulating her on purchasing Hamdown, in rural East Wellow, near Romsey, in Hampshire. He said she 'certainly could not have chosen a more lovely spot and I thought the house was so nice.'[197]

Although a manager at the pottery it was clear where his sympathies lay, and his political awareness gradually grew. In another letter to his mother he writes, 'The pay is often wicked for the amount of work exacted, and such work illuminates the under-nourished condition of the working girls, as they get struck down with colds and flu very easily. Their clothes too, are often much too thin. Yet even under such conditions we get in a lot of fun; though it makes me socialist'.[198]

The war in Spain then loomed large, and by then Herbert had joined the Communist Party. He set off in November 1937 saying simply, 'I am just off to fight for the People in Spain' and entered the British Battalion on 2 December 1937.[199] His many letters home show a great spirit, and a joy at joining the Spanish people in their fight against fascism. Even learning Spanish was not a problem because it 'is easy as it is so like Latin.'

Letters from the Potteries and Spain.

HERBERT DOUGLAS FISHER,
b. 1910; Dragon School, 1920-24; King Williams'
College, Isle of Man, 1924-29. For three years ap-
prentice Peter Potters, Ashtead, Surrey. Afterwards
Departmental Manager in two pottery firms at Stoke-
on-Trent. Joined the International Brigade in Spain
November, 1937. Joined the British Battalion on the
Aragon front February 12th, 1938; reported missing
March 18th, 1938.

Herbert Fisher
Courtesy Dragon School magazine 'The Draconian', April 1939

In another letter, dated 12 December 1937, he gave an indication of the difficulties the Spanish government had in properly arming their forces, 'Since I have been here, besides having a few rifles for demonstration purposes and firing practices, we have been issued with wooden rifles for every day drill.' Two days later another letter showed his grim determination to fight the evil of fascism, 'For me the fight has shifted from the Potteries to Spain. I am not concerned with one opinion alone; for all opinion, freedom of speech and democracy for the majority is fighting for its very life and existence.'[200]

He expanded on this in a letter dated 9 January, 'The plain truth is this: since the Fascist is a man who does not follow ordinary democratic rules, it is impossible to resist him in a democratic way. Therefore prompt, ruthless action is needed. It is stupid that I have to waste time in saying this when it seems so obvious.'

Herbert's final letter home was dated late February 1938 as his company was moved up the line.[201] On 9 March the fascists launched their massive offensive which smashed through the Republican Government lines, forcing the British Battalion, and their International and Spanish comrades, to retreat right through Aragon with massive losses.

Herbert and so many others were never seen again, either killed in the battle, shot out of hand when surrendering, or trying to swim the River Ebro to the safety of the new front line. The record keeping of the British Battalion was never consistent, even in peaceful times, but faced with the chaos of the retreats, the very long wait to see how many would make it back, or to receive lists of prisoners, it would take many months before relatives could be given some certainty about the fate of their missing relatives in Spain.

For Herbert's mother, Janie, the pain of not knowing would last longer than most. In the confusion, Herbert's records became conflated with John Herbert Fisher, a commercial traveller from London. He had also fought in Aragon, and went on to be wounded at the Battle of the Ebro. Desperate for news, Janie used her brother-in-law, H.A.L. Fisher, to lobby the Foreign Secretary Viscount Halifax. He reported back that the fascists had confirmed Herbert was not on any prisoner list.[202] She then lobbied the Dependants and Wounded Aid Committee in London for news, but in response they simply perpetuated the mistake that he was possibly in hospital in Santa Coloma.[203]

Finally, Janie took a plaintive small add out in the Daily Worker to coincide with the return of the bulk of the British Brigaders asking for 'any comrade who may have known' Herbert to get in touch.[204] Eventually, she received a letter from John Penman, a Fife miner who had travelled out to Spain and over the Pyrenees with Herbert. He was taken prisoner at Calaceite on 31 March 1938 and wrote a year later, after being released. He went up the line a week after Herbert, and said that when he joined the Battalion he made enquiries about him, 'from some of the fellows who knew him, and was told by several he had been killed somewhere between Belchite and Caspe between 10 and 17 March. Nobody could tell me how he died as no one was actually with him.'

Interestingly it was not only John Herbert who was confused with Herbert. American volunteer Harry Fisher, who fought with the Abraham Lincoln Battalion, recalled that just before he was repatriated, 'when the retreats were over . . . One day a huge package was delivered to me from England. I opened it wondering who in England could have sent it. I spoke to Johnny Power who told me that there was an Englishman named Harry Fisher (Herbert) who had been killed some months earlier. Johnny had known him, and said he was a good Comrade, and no doubt about it, he would have wanted me to keep the package.'[205][206]

73

William Thomas George Beales (1910-1938)

The overwhelming majority of the British volunteers to the International Brigades in Spain knew exactly why they were there, and the importance of the battle in front of them. However, it is also the case that the war attracted a number of men for a multitude of other reasons, some thinking it would be glamourous or some simply escaping their life in the UK. It is likely that William Beales fell into this latter category.

William was born on 13 January 1910, in a common lodging house at 9 Staffordshire Street, Cambridge. His father Robert was a general labourer, and mother Rosetta would be a widow for the third time just two years later.

Little more is known about William. He entered Spain on 9 December 1937, giving his job as Road Locomotive Driver. When he enlisted he gave his contact name as Edith Pollinger, landlady at The Eagle, 32 High Street, Newport, on the Isle of Wight.

However, there is one intriguing episode that suggests it was not a spur of the moment decision to go to Spain. A newspaper report details how he and two friends were arrested in France, whilst 'walking to Paris', in March 1937.[207] They were charged with vagrancy and sentenced to fifteen days in prison. Certainly the UK security services considered them probable recruits to the International Brigades as they were added to their files.[208] There is also a note about William leaving for Spain again on 28 November 1937.

The one report of him during his time in Spain suggests that he did not take to soldiering well, with a 'consistent opposition to command.'[209] However, along with Herbert Fisher, who arrived in Spain around the same time, he was in Company 5 of the XV International Brigade, when they were thrown into the front line to try and stem the advance of the fascists through Aragon in March 1938.[210] Both were eventually declared missing, presumed dead.

Douglas Copleston Eggar (1900-1992)

Douglas Eggar was born in Eton, on 29 December 1900, the eldest of five children of an Eton schoolmaster. By 1911 he was a boarder at Bigshotte Rayles Preparatory School in Wokingham and his secondary education was spent at Eton.[211]

He spent two years in the Hampshire Regiment as a soldier from 1919-1921, after which he went to King's College London for two years to study theology. He then headed for the West Indies as a 'planter' in October 1923. This was a short lived venture and he returned to the UK in March 1925. By this time his father had retired from Eton and returned to his own birthplace of Bentley, near Alton, in Hampshire, where his grandfather had owned a substantial farm.

Douglas's next major career move was as a Metropolitan Police Officer, serving from January 1927 until December 1936, living variously in Camberwell, Grays Inn Road and Holborn.[212] He retired as 'unfit', following a football injury, but was retained as a messenger. His interest in politics was sparked by involvement in the protests against the framing, and execution, of the American anarchists Sacco and Vanzetti, and he was influenced by the writers Upton Sinclair and Sinclair Lewis.

He was also moved by the life and death of intellectual and poet John Cornford in Spain, and unsuccessfully tried to get to Spain firstly as an ambulance driver and then as an International Brigader.[213] By this time he had forged a friendship with Esmond Romilly, who had fought with Ray Cox at Boadilla, and it was on his assurance that he was finally permitted to travel to Spain.

He arrived in Spain, via Espola, on 4 January 1938, and was formally enrolled in the British Battalion on 11 January.[214] [215] The address he gave was in Exmouth, Devon, where his maternal grandfather was a vicar. His police connection meant that his name found itself on lists of Brigaders who were 'bad elements' or 'suspects, where he was damned with being accused of having 'liberal democratic tendencies', although one annotation reads 'ex policeman but seems ok.' [216] [217]

Douglas is listed as being at Battalion Base on 13 February 1938 but by the end of March he had been caught up in the chaos of the retreats through Aragon and taken prisoner, being held in the notorious San Pedro de Cardeña Prison. He was released and repatriated in October 1938. [218] [219]

In 1939 Douglas was living in Great Ormond Street, London and working as a War Reserve Police Officer. After the war he had a variety of jobs including being a police messenger and gardener. Known to his family as Dougal, he was regarded by his family as a kind and gentle man, with a lot of friends, who was particularly good to his nieces.[220] He died in Lambeth on 22 April 1992, with his funeral service taking place in St. Luke's Church, Peckham. The order of service included 'The Song of the International Brigades' and 'The Valley of Jarama'. Following an address by Bill Alexander, former Commander of the British Battalion in Spain, the service was played out to the 'Internationale'. Douglas is buried in St. Mary's Churchyard in the Hampshire village of Bentley.

George Alexander Robertson (1914-1954)

George Robertson was born in Aldershot, Hampshire, on 3 December 1914, his father a Piper with the 1st Battalion of the famous Black Watch. At some stage the family moved to 38 Carrick Knowe, Edinburgh. After school George became a mechanic/driver and joined the Young Communist League.

He married in October 1935, a decision which was to prove fateful. He arrived in Spain on 22 October 1937 just three months after the birth of his second child, giving his mother as his contact. An indication of his state of mind was suggested by fellow Scottish Brigader Tommy Broomfield who wrote that he had 'lived rough and they thought he was a drunkard and a lazy sort, but he was a braw soldier in Spain'.[221] Indeed the only note about him in the Moscow archives notes that he was 'only interested in reading, disciplined, good politics, good morale.'[222] Maybe he was simply able to find some peace of mind so far from his domestic situation.

Like so many of the British Battalion he was caught up in the retreats through Aragon in March 1938. He was originally reported missing but found to be wounded, and he spent a period in the hospital at Santa Coloma, before being repatriated on 25 October 1938.

It is unclear what he was doing during World War Two, but immediately afterwards he seems to have embarked on a criminal career. In April 1945 he was imprisoned for two years for theft, followed in September 1947 with a four year term of penal servitude for crimes including robbery, violence, and the possession of explosives.[223] [224] During his second term of imprisonment 1948 he divorced, and his wife remarried in 1950, although this marriage quickly foundered. In April 1951 he received another three year term for housebreaking and theft.[225] Shortly after his release he was arrested and charged with drink driving on 4 January 1954.

On 28 February 1954 things came to a head, after he broke into his ex-wife's house and brutally murdered her and their eighteen year old son, also seriously wounding his sixteen year old daughter.[226] He only spoke after being found guilty, at the end of a two day trial, when he asked the Judge if the powers that be could not amend the law so that 'men in my position' could be allowed to plead guilty and avoid the formality of a trial, thus sparing everyone's time and feelings.[227]

George Robertson
Courtesy Edinburgh Evening News, 1 March 1954

George Robertson became the last person to be executed in Edinburgh Prison, on 23 June 1954. His cause of death is recorded as 'Judicial Hanging'.

Arthur Richard Lydiard Moss (1912-1938)

More commonly known as Richard or Dick, Arthur Moss was born in Katihar, Bihar, India, on 28 March 1912, the son of a British railway engineer. He was educated as a boarder at the Catholic Ampleforth Prep School in Yorkshire, from 1926-1929.

From Ampleforth, Richard went to Trinity College, Dublin, in 1930-1932. It is believed in the family that his time at Trinity was not a happy one, and that he dropped out some time after a fracas that followed a veterans' march through the city.[228] The family embarrassment would have been heightened by the fact that his grandfather, Richard Jackson Moss, was the Registrar of the Royal Dublin Society from 1878 to 1920, and the family home was St Aubyns, in Ballybrack, Co Dublin.

He studied chemistry at Imperial College London from 1934-35, before going on to study physiology at University College, London in 1935. He left in 1937 without completing the course. About this time his parents retired, returning from India and moving into Landour, Connaught Road, Fleet, Hampshire.

On 13 January 1934 he married Eileen Josephine Hennessy, at St Mary of the Angels, Paddington. In November 1935 he was charged with 'wilfully damaging the wall of the Convent of the Poor Clare, in Cornwall Road, North Kensington.'[229] Using white distemper 'he painted the words "Daily Worker" in large letters on the wall'.[230] The charge was dismissed on payment of compensation for the damage.

Now living at Ladbroke Grove in London, and described as an 'excellent comrade' of the West Kensington Branch of the Communist Party, Richard arrived in Spain on 22 February 1938.[231] He was placed in the 3rd Company of the XX International Brigade. Tragically for him he arrived immediately before the fascists launched their offensive through Aragon. He was declared 'missing after his first action' on 3 April 1938 near Caspe.[232] He was machine-gunned, his death being witnessed by fellow Londoner Harold Collins.[233]

Like so many others, confusion over his exact name and doubts about witness reports led to a long period of uncertainty as to his fate. His mother wrote to Foreign Secretary Lord Halifax, on two occasions.[234] He replied on 2 February 1939 to say that Richard was not on the lists of British prisoners remaining in Spain. His widow Eileen returned to her family home in Ireland, but sadly died of tuberculosis in Dublin on 4 December 1946.

Dick Moss – Courtesy of Simon Theobalds

Henry Johnson aka Lionel Leslie East
(1907-   )

Henry Johnson was born on 11 September 1907 in the family home at 42 Victoria Road, Aldershot, the third of four children of a Master Baker. Aged just seventeen he migrated to Australia, arriving in Queensland in July 1925. He worked as a truck driver and mechanic and served two years in the Australian Militia, along with joining the Australian Workers Union and the Communist Party of Australia.[235] [236] [237]

He went to Spain via London in March 1938. Commenting on his reason for going he said, 'It was the only thing a decent man could do who hated tyranny'.[238] For reasons still unknown, he had adopted the alias of Lionel Leslie East and a birth date of 16 December 1910. The real Leslie East lived close to the family home in Aldershot, and his date of birth was 16 December 1911.

Henry/Lionel arrived on 6 March 1938, just as the fascist onslaught through Aragon was launched. Part of a machine gun crew, he explained how, like so many others, they 'were cut off in the big attack at the beginning of April'.[239] After spending eight days trying to get back to the Government lines he was taken prisoner. Fortunately, unlike so many of his international comrades, he was not simply shot on sight. He then spent a miserable few months in the notorious San Pedro de Cardeña Prison near Burgos before being part of a group released in a prisoner exchange for captured fascist Italian soldiers.

Having arrived back in the UK it was clear Henry/Lionel was keen to return to Australia, the extraordinary tale of how he achieved this was recounted by Australian author Amirah Inglis. It involved Albert Robinson, a seaman from Sydney, who had been badly wounded in the hand at the Battle of the Ebro. Robinson had decided to enter the Middlesex hospital for another operation on his hand, but when the 'Orion' sailed from London on 28 January 1939 his name was on the passenger list. It turned out he had given his ticket and identity to Henry/Lionel. This caused something of a diplomatic incident until the Australian Prime Minister's office contacted the ship to confirm that if East 'was an International Brigader, no action'. And there the story ends. Lionel East as Robinson landed in Australia and melted away.[240]

John William Charles (1913-1979)

John Charles – Courtesy of Rosa Branson

John Charles was born in the family home at 52 Canada Road, Woolston, Southampton, on 22 February 1913, the house where he lived for all but the last three years of his life. His sister was born a year later but, meanwhile, his marine engineer father had answered the call to arms and was killed at Gallipoli, in 1915, at the age of 35. Tragically his mother was also to die in 1922 leaving the two young children to be brought up by an aunt.[241]

At the time of going to Spain John was working as a skilled aircraft fitter and, apart from being a member of the Amalgamated Engineering Union, which would have gone with the job, there is no evidence of any political activity. It is believed he was driven to go to Spain after listening to the stories of the Basque children refugees, at the camp in nearby Stoneham, where volunteers like him, did everything from digging drains to providing the meals. He arrived in Spain on the day before his twenty-fifth birthday in February 1938. By the end of April he was already in the notorious San Pedro de Cardeña prison near Burgos, having been captured during the retreats through Aragon. He was released and repatriated in October 1938.

After returning from Spain he returned to his reserved occupation as an aircraft fitter, but was also a part time firemen during the terrible blitz of Southampton in World War Two. After the war he went to work as a stevedore in Southampton Docks, joining the Transport & General Workers Union, whose later General Secretary Jack Jones, had also fought and been wounded in Spain.

Marriage in 1941 produced four sons and a daughter. John enjoyed his hobby as a racing pigeon fancier with son Malcolm, and was also an accomplished amateur footballer, playing in goal. Another son, Bob, followed in his father's footsteps as a goalkeeper and had a brief career with Southampton Football Club. John died in Southampton on 10 May 1979.

Chapter Eight

July/August 1938—The Battle of the Ebro

In late July 1938 the Government launched a well-planned surprise offensive across the River Ebro, in order to try and push the fascists back. After a lot of early success the advance gradually got bogged down, and eventually petered out. Once again the crucial factor was the shortage of planes and artillery, as result of the Non-Intervention Treaty.

David Leslie Goldsmid Haden-Guest (1911-1938)

David Guest was born in the Adelphi, London, on 6 January 1911, where the elder Disraeli had written the 'Curiosities of Literature'.[242] His father, Leslie, was Medical Superintendent at a pioneering school clinic, and a recognised author, journalist, social reformer, and politician. From 1933-1950 he was elected as the Member of Parliament for North Islington, and was later ennobled as a Baron in the House of Lords. David's mother, Muriel Carmel, was a successful playwright and author.

Although David hated his time at prep school, he continued to develop his early interest in science and politics. His brother Peter recalled how a Headteacher wrote in a report when he was just ten, 'He has such an active brain that I am sometimes terrified.'[243] Sixth form, from 1927-29, was at Oundle public school in Northamptonshire, and then it was on to Trinity College, Cambridge, where he graduated with a first class honours degree in mathematics in 1932.

At Trinity David was able to pursue his great interest in

David Guest punting at Cambridge
Courtesy of Christopher Haden-Guest

mathematical philosophy which included attending lectures by the great philosopher Wittgenstein. This led to his second year being spent largely at Gottingen University in Germany, home of the famous mathematician Hilbert and one of the most renowned centres for mathematical teaching and research. Whilst he thrived academically, his position also allowed him to see at first hand the increasing Nazification of Germany.

His observations drew him to increasingly believe that only Communism could provide an economic system that would not engineer the inequalities dictated by Capitalism, which provided a breeding ground for Fascism. He wrote, 'In the long run the argument between socialism and Capitalism is precisely the argument which has run through the whole course of human history—may we, without impiety to the Gods, use our intellect? May we obtain control of our environment and of our destiny—or should we humbly be content to live like the other animals without too much thinking.'[244]

David's political education was taken a stage further when he attended a youth demonstration on Easter Sunday 1931. He was arrested along with over 400 other young people and spent two uncomfortable and frightening weeks in prison as a result. Despite his frail physique which was a constant concern for family and friends, this experience merely spurred on his desire to effect change and to challenge fascism and soon after his return to England he was involved in another demonstration. On this occasion it was protesting against unemployment outside the House of Commons. It attracted the usual heavy handed police response to any to left wing demonstration, and resulted in not only David being arrested for insulting behaviour, but also his mother for obstructing the police. At Bow Street Magistrates Court she protested that she 'only intervened to prevent her son being marched away', but this was to no avail as they were both bound over for twelve months.[245] During this period David also formally joined the Communist Party and was one of the leaders of the Cambridge University Socialist Society.

After leaving University in the summer of 1933 he moved into lodgings in Battersea, London, with Herbert Sines and his family, again vociferously supporting the cause of the unemployed. From there he left to teach for a year at the Anglo-American school in Moscow which provided a stimulating break from the intensive activity he had been involved in at home. On his return, he volunteered his talents to the Marx Memorial Library and Workers School, in Clerkenwell, London. Along with lecturing, tutoring, and other roles, he was also continuing his mathematical research at the University of London, along with supporting the activities of the Young Communist League. Such was his output whilst lecturing at the Marx Memorial Worker's School, his lecture notes and correspondence were published after his death in 'A Text Book of Dialectical Materialism.'

Another project was the establishment of a 'People's Bookshop' in Lavender Hill, London. This naturally meant joining the Shop Assistants Union (SAU), where he also took an active role. At around the same time he made another court appearance resulting from a clash with fascists on Clapham Common. Accompanied in the dock by his friend Herbert Sines, he was charged with insulting behaviour and assaulting a Police Officer, for which he was duly fined ten shillings (50p).[246]

From October 1937 to March 1938 he was a lecturer in mathematics at the University College of Southampton (now Southampton University). Despite only being there for two terms he clearly left his mark. Part of his obituary in the University student newspaper read, 'He will be remembered for his great intellectual brilliance, for his friendly disposition, for his intense devotion to the social betterment of mankind, and, not least, for the sense of humour that enlivened even the most serious of the philosophical and political discussions in which he was ever engaged. It is especially tragic that one who worked so hard for peace and who cared so much for orderly and enlightened government should have lost his life in war.'[247]

Whilst at Southampton University he was also active in the University Socialist Society and Left Book Club along with his work for the Communist Party which included speaking engagements.[248] On the eve of leaving for Spain he addressed a meeting arranged by Portsmouth Labour League of Youth in the Trades Hall. He did not mention his intention to go to Spain but concentrated on the short sighted attitude of the British Government and the policy of non-intervention. He argued that, 'even from a purely Imperialist point of view the attitude of the National Government was a suicidal one. It passively stood by or indeed encouraged the encirclement of the Empire and the cutting of lines of communications by Fascist Powers, all of whom were greedy for colonial expansion.'[249]

His decision to go to Spain was not taken on the spur of the moment, and amongst his papers was one entitled 'Reasons for my Decision' in which he wrote 'Today we have certainly entered a period of crisis, when the arguments of 'normal times' no longer apply, when considerations of most usefulness come in.[250] That is why I have decided to take the opportunity of going to Spain. It is true that during my short stay at Southampton I might have been able to do a certain amount of good work, and might be able to do still more. However, a great deal of my time would continue to be taken up by routine mathematical work (teaching), and the very growth of ordinary political work would make it Utopian to expect to do much philosophy and mathematical logic . . . Finally I believe that the experience of the struggle will give me just those qualities of practical life that I lack. My short experience of University life was useful. But in a world of wars and revolutions new tasks are on the agenda. Let us see they are carried out.'

Amongst those who accompanied David on the trip down through France and across the Pyrenees to Spain was Herbert Sines. This was his second journey to Spain. He had previously arrived in Spain in December 1936, and was wounded in the bloody Battle of Jarama and invalided home. This experience, along with friends from Cambridge and

Battersea, who had already been killed in Spain, meant that David would have been under no illusions about what might happen to him.

He arrived on 29 March 1938 quickly taking on additional roles to that of simply being an infantryman. These included becoming secretary of the United Socialist Youth, encouraging political thought and discussion amongst the younger soldiers, internationals and Spanish alike. His skills as a mathematician also made him an ideal candidate for the highly dangerous role of forward observer. It was in this role for No 2 Company of the British Battalion that he entered the battle of the Ebro until 26 July 1938 and was shot near Gandesa by a 'Moorish sniper.' Commander of the British Battalion Sam Wild recounted how 'he fell in an advanced position of his company. He was reconnoitring the terrain for the possible means of approach to this important enemy position which our battalion had to attack. He died as he lived, fighting against fascism which symbolises oppression and reaction in its worst form.'[251]

Following his death there was a huge march and memorial service to remember him, along with fellow volunteer Tom Oldershaw. His devoted mother, who visited David in Spain, twice, later wrote to the local paper thanking everybody saying, 'He would have been immeasurably moved had he known of the memorial march and meeting in Battersea in which vast numbers united to honour Tom Oldershaw and him, and through them, their comrades in the International Brigade, who have given their lives for liberty. The message of David's intensely active life and tragically early death is that we must redouble our efforts in the fight against Fascism, and to those of us who knew him intimately, and love and weep for him, he would say now, and he said to the boys who picked him up, mortally wounded in the Ebro advance, "Don't worry about me comrades, go on." '[252]

Charles Adshead Saunders (1906-1979)

Charlie Saunders was born in Portsmouth on 24 October 1906, the third of six children. His father was a Chief Petty Officer in the Royal Navy whose ship was sunk in 1918 leaving him wounded, and earning him the Distinguished Service Medal. After school Charlie began the search for work, which included a year of a plumbing apprenticeship at Crampton & Co.'s shipbuilding yard in Landport, Portsmouth.[253]

Like so many other young men of the period the pursuit of work and a better life led him to emigrate, and he arrived on the ship 'Penland' in Halifax, Nova Scotia, Canada, on 27 March 1927. He found work farming and as a logger, but the economic depression which had driven so many to Canada soon caught up with him there. For Charlie and 170,248 others it meant a long spell in one of the so called Nationwide Relief Camps.[254] During this time he joined the Vancouver Branch of the Communist Party of Canada (CPC) which led the opposition to the camps.

His impressive record of industrial struggles saw his participation in strikes by the Longshoremen and the Burns Packing Plant in Vancouver and involvement in the Relief Project Workers Union.[255] He was also a member of the 'Writers Group of the Progressive Arts Club' in Vancouver, where he also wrote articles for the Communist Party paper.[256]

Charlie left Canada for Spain on 10 May 1937, arriving on 10 August. He gave his mother as his contact, and the address was that of his grandmother, at 32 Clifton Road, Winchester, where his now widowed mother was also living. Charlie was one of around 1,681 Canadians who went to Spain, over 400 of whom never returned.[257] His arrival coincided with enough other Canadians to enable the formation of the Mackenzie-Papineau (Mac-Paps) Battalion within the XVI International Brigade.[258] His courage and leadership qualities must have been obvious from the start, as he was soon sent for training for the highly dangerous job as a Brigade scout.[259]

He saw action at Fuentes de Ebro during the battle for Teruel, after which he was promoted to the rank of Sergeant.[260] In his new role as Sergeant Platoon Leader he fought at Gandesa and was wounded in the bloody attack on Hill 481 in the Sierra Pandolls, during the Battle of the Ebro, on 28 July 1938. His recovery from a wound in his right thigh took two months to heal, and coincided with the withdrawal of the International Brigades.[261]

Charles Saunders (October 1936) – Courtesy of John Biles

After a lot of prevarication by the Canadian Government the majority of Mac-Paps left in Spain returned to Canada on 11 February 1939. Charlie left Spain with a glowing report of his military and political conduct. An assessment was made by Party Leaders on his departure from Spain which stated: 'Prospects: a propaganda writer.'[262]

Whilst they might have thought the conflict was over for them, one perpetual enemy who would not be shaken off was discovered by Charlie after he had a morning wash, in the back of a tourist coach heading to Vancouver.[263] He returned to his seat next to fellow Brigader Ronald Liversedge and remarked that, 'While I was washing back there I found four of the biggest, fattest lice, I have ever seen, in my undershirt.'

Known as Chuck back home, he returned to work as a militant member of the International Woodworkers of America, working as a union Business Agent.[264]

He moved from North Vancouver to Cranbrook, British Columbia, where he married and had a son, and passing away on 29 November 1979.

Stanley Israel Harrison aka Brentman (1917-1985)

Stan Harrison was born on 16 April 1917, in Southwark, London, the son of a Jewish tailor and shopkeeper, Aaron Breitelman.[265] His father had arrived in England in around 1900 as the result of fleeing the Jewish pogroms in Ukraine and other parts of the Czarist Russian Empire.[266] The name Harrison was adopted after a signwriter was struggling with the name Breitelman and suggested using his name, Harrison, which might also avoid the anti-Semitism rife in England at the time and be better for business.

During Stan's childhood the family lived at a number of

addresses in London, Southampton and Portsmouth. While in Southampton he attended Taunton's School from 1928-31, and then Southern School in Portsmouth.[267] Family finances meant that University was not an option, so he left school at sixteen and worked as a junior reporter for the Hants & Sussex County Press, and then for the Salisbury Journal. He was subsequently taken on by the Portsmouth Evening News as their reporter for the Isle of Wight. Having already become an active member of the National Union of Journalists and being elected Father of the Chapel, and also the Communist Party, his politics were at odds with the right wing stance of the newspaper and a pretext was found to fire him.[268]

His anti-fascism naturally took him to Spain where he arrived on 18 April 1938. Having made the arduous trip through France, with an overnight trek over the Pyrenees, he was almost turned around and sent straight back home due to his poor eyesight, which made him unacceptable for a combat role. However, after a heartfelt plea to the British Battalion Commissar, Michael Economides, to be allowed to have some role in the fight against fascism, he was accepted as a stretcher bearer with the British Battalion.

On 25 July 1938, he was moved across the River Ebro in a rowing boat along with the rest of the Battalion to join in the last major attempt to break the continued fascist advance. The job of a stretcher bearer was fraught with danger and difficulty. It was a long haul over difficult terrain in order to get casualties back to the boats to ferry them to safety, and treatment. Stan described what happened after crossing the Ebro: 'We were very rapidly brought in touch with the situation because anything that moved along the banks of the Ebro was subjected to strafing and machine-gunning from the air and bombing and shelling by artillery. This even applied to the wounded. We were carrying wounded back to the banks of the river and getting them on to the boats to be rowed across for medical aid, as there were of course on the enemy side of the river no facilities for treating casualties. We stretcher bearers were obliged on many occasions to take cover with our patients or to cover the wounded with our own bodies to save them being caught by machine gun fire from the air. This I think was the first incident of strafing which was a German word which came into force at that time and was to be heard a lot more during the Second World War . . .

When we were carrying wounded soldiers during the Ebro offensive one of the most heart-breaking things that used to happen to us stretcher bearers was, when we jolted them in any way the wounded men would respond with cries of anguish and pain, but in the case of the Spanish wounded they always called 'mi Madre' these young Spanish soldiers would always call for their mother if they were really hurt.

It was our unfortunate duty to the point of departure to cross the river to the hospital. We were obliged to harden our hearts and to get them on their way, regardless of any pain and suffering we caused in the process. I don't think it is possible to be a medical ancillary unless you can force yourself to harden your heart and not to feel as deeply as you did feel. You have a job to do and you had to get on with that job and if any pain is caused as a result of your actions it cannot be your fault. We were obliged to get those wounded across the river.'

The strain of carrying and lifting stretchers eventually caused Stan internal injuries which meant a spell in hospital in Mataró for an operation and recuperation. Whilst in hospital he got word of the death of David Guest who he had known from his Communist Party activities in Hampshire, They had bumped into each other at Battalion Headquarters, both surprised to see each other. He visited David's mother on returning home, and found that she was very distraught at both David's loss and the fact there would be no grave for her to visit.

FILIACION

Estatura

Pelo

Ojos

Cara

Barba

Nariz
SEÑAS PARTICULARES

(Firma del interesado)

Fecha de nacimiento ___ 16. 4 1917

Lugar de nacimiento ___ Londres

Nacionalidad ___ Inglés

Profesión ___ Periodista

Estado civil ___ Soltero

DOMICILIO: País ___ Inglaterra

Pueblo ___ Poorts menth

Calle ___ Gains Road ___ núm. 44

Partido Político ___ Antifascista

Fecha de entrada en las B. I. ___ 26 5 1938

Fecha de entrega de la libreta ___ 8 10 1938

— 2 —

Stan Harrison's Paybook – Courtesy of Rosalyn Fowler

By the time Stan had recovered the Spanish Government had withdrawn the International Brigades from action, and he was assembled at Ripoli with the rest of the British Battalion, prior to their repatriation to London on 8 December 1938.

The lengthy wait for repatriation, after their withdrawal from active service, was largely due to foot-dragging by the British Government in supplying the necessary paperwork. Their exasperation was expressed in a letter written by Stan, and jointly signed by fellow Portsmouth British Brigader George Burton, to his local paper.[269] They complained that, 'We have been out of the line for over two months, and many of us have been out here fighting for democracy for periods up to two years, separated from our families whom we are naturally anxious to see again as soon as possible.' They urged 'that all the democrats of Portsmouth take up this matter with our three Members of Parliament.'

On his return Stan immediately wrote again to the paper lauding the 'tremendous welcome by the people of London, and later, the members of the Battalion received individual welcomes in their various home towns and villages.'[270] He explained that the British Consul in Ripoli only finally facilitated their return after the British Battalion had 'threatened to march over the French border as a Battalion' with all the resulting publicity that would have entailed. He also made a plea for the Portsmouth Members of Parliament to raise the plight of the Canadian Mac-Paps Battalion, whose Government was proving even more obstructive in enabling their return than the British Government had been with their citizens.

It was around this time that Stan also reverted back to using his family's correct surname, albeit with the slightly anglicized spelling of Brentman. What was happening to Jews in Germany was already well known to those who were politically aware, although the British establishment was happy to turn a blind eye, so it was normal practice for British Brigaders with surnames of Jewish origin to adopt an alias in Spain as there was a fear that, if taken prisoner in Spain, they would be handed over to the Nazis.

Early in 1939 a group of British Brigaders took part in a

nationwide speaking tour to raise public awareness of the plight of the Spanish people and the need to revoke the Non-Intervention Treaty, and also to raise funds to send food. Their first port of call was Portsmouth and Stan was given the job of organising the meeting. In a letter to Bill Alexander he explained how every attempt was made to ensure it was 'as broad-based as possible.' [271] This meant inviting an old Colonel to chair the meeting, who rapidly agreed and said he would make the arrangements in a church hall in Fratton Road, Portsmouth. Stan was both surprised and alarmed when he turned up on the evening of the meeting to find hymn sheets on every chair and a programme which included the National Anthem. He was particularly concerned about what the final leader of the British Battalion, Sam Wild, and the main speaker, final Battalion Commissar Bob Cooney, would make of it. However, John Peet, another British Brigader who was in attendance, recounted that the 'Brigaders on the platform wondered what to do, but Bob Cooney saved the situation by springing to attention and leading the singing of all three verses (of the national anthem) to the astonishment of the mainly left audience, but discipline prevailed.'[272]

Stan continued to write to the local paper in Portsmouth, trying to alert the population at large of the threat posed by the spread of Fascism, and the desperate need to end the phony policy of non-intervention. He ended one letter by warning, 'The big guns can be heard in that wonderful city of Barcelona now. In order that they may never be heard in London or Portsmouth, we should see that the disastrous policy pursued by Britain since the outbreak of this war is reversed, and that the Spanish Government gets the arms for which it can afford to pay'.[273]

After a short break, he went to work as the Press Officer for Sir Stafford Cripps MP, who was heading the campaign to persuade the left to unite in a Popular Front to confront the evil of fascism. Cripps's efforts were met with expulsion from the Labour Party, so Stan began working as a freelance journalist in Fleet Street. Despite his best efforts, he was once again rejected for military service, in World War Two on health grounds. So began a long career with a number of major newspapers including the News Chronicle, Observer, Jewish Gazette and Daily Telegraph. He took early retirement from the Telegraph after symptoms of Parkinson's disease made travelling and working difficult.

Stan had married in July 1945. Just before his death on 15 December 1985 at his Ruby wedding anniversary, he was delighted to have his friend Michael Economides as a guest, the comrade who allowed him to stay and play a part in fighting fascism in Spain.

Herbert Henry Albert Hartwell (1910-1991)

Herbert Hartwell was born on 16 February 1910 in Brockhurst, Gosport, though even in later life, Herbert usually wrote his year of birth as 1909, as his father had altered his birth certificate in order that he could leave school and start work at thirteen years old instead of fourteen.[274]

Herbert's mother sadly died in 1914 and, at some stage after his father had been demobbed as a stoker from the Royal Navy in 1919, they moved to Derbyshire.[275] Herbert was soon at work as a miner, first at 'B' Winning and then at Blackwell pit. The economic depression and lack of work soon drew him into politics, and he joined the National Unemployed Workers Movement and went on one of the National Hunger Marches after joining the Communist Party in 1936.[276] [277]

Although, by now, he was married with a young son he could not resist the call to 'fight fascism, save democracy' in Spain.[278] He was an ideal recruit for the International Brigade as he had served four years in the Territorial Army, with the

5th Battalion of the Sherwood Foresters in Derbyshire, and with his friend Horace Windle, they left to fight at the end of January 1938.[279]

They arrived on 7 February 1938 and, after training, Herbert was assigned to No 4 Company of the British Battalion. Along with the rest of the battalion, he was soon caught up in the huge fascist offensive through Aragon. By the time he had made his way back through enemy lines and re-joined the British Battalion he had been posted as missing, and added to a list of possible prisoners.[280]

He next saw action at the battle of the Ebro.[281] Previously having been a runner for Company Commander Paddy O'Daire, he was utilised as a stretcher bearer, where he proved to be extremely brave in what was a very dangerous role.[282] He was repatriated back to Britain on 22 December 1938, serving to the last, helping to care for the sick and wounded on the hospital train back to London.

Back in Normanton he was initially blacklisted because of his politics, but was eventually able to regain his job as a miner. Herbert died in November 1991. He ended his autobiography, *The Lost Weekend*, by saying, 'The Fascists were well equipped. They sent crack troops out there. We thinned 'em out before the British army took 'em on in World War Two. If they'd given us the equipment there might not have been World War Two. I've never regretted going.'[283]

James Arthur Moore (1916-1939)

Jimmy Moore was born in Princes Street, Edinburgh, on 19 September 1916, but it was not long before the economic depression drove the family to move to Portsmouth in search of work. After leaving school Jimmy went to work in the Naval Dockyard as an electrician's mate. He was an active member of the Transport & General Workers Union (TGWU) and represented his Branch on Portsmouth Trades Council.

We do not know precisely where his politics lay, as in his Battalion questionnaire he wrote, 'owing to my job I was unable to join working class organisations.'[284] He left the family home at 52 Belmont Street, Southsea, Portsmouth, and arrived in Spain on 15 June 1938. After training he was assigned to No 1 Company of the XV Brigade and the now 57th Battalion, just in time to be thrown into the Battle of the Ebro with the rest of the British Battalion. He was seriously wounded in the 'leg and back by a fascist shell' in an attack on Hill 666 in the Sierra Pandolls on 22 August 1938.[285]

Jimmy spent the rest of his time in Spain in hospital, including six weeks in Villa Franca and another six weeks in Vich. Sadly, an infection set into his leg wound and his condition deteriorated. However, it appears his spirit and optimism never diminished, he wrote on 20 November that he envisaged 'a great future for the Spanish people when fascism is defeated.'[286]

In a letter to his local newspaper he wrote, 'Although we volunteers are leaving Spain, the fight against Fascism is not finished. The Republican Government now faces one of the hardest times of the war, through the lack of support from Democratic Governments. The most urgent requirements at present are food, clothing and medical supplies. I myself being in hospital through being hit by shrapnel from a shell, can see the great need for medical supplies. Owing to the lack of these supplies the wounded cannot receive the attention that is needed for their complete recovery, and I believe if the people of Portsmouth only knew the true conditions in Spain, they would rally together, with the other people of England, to see that the embargo was lifted from Republican Spain, and allow them to exterminate these Fascist invaders.'[287]

He continued, 'Although I have not been in Spain long, I shall always feel proud of having stood shoulder to shoulder with these heroic people in their fight for existence from the

Fascist regime'.

On 6 December 1938 most of the British Battalion returned home. Two weeks later the sixty-nine sick and wounded were put on a train which had been adapted as an ambulance, and given an emotional farewell by the local Spanish people.

As a final betrayal, or in an act of sheer spite towards the cause the injured Brigaders had championed (which would envelop Europe within 12 months), the British Government required them to sign a 'Repatriation' form pledging to repay the Government for the cost of their return home.[288]

Those attending them on the train included Dr Harry Bury, and David Guest's sister, Angela. Despite their care, the bitterly cold weather meant that some of the wounded were frost bitten by the time they reached Paris.[289] Five, including Jimmy, were so seriously ill they were taken from the train to the Hartford British Hospital in Paris, to try and stabilise their conditions. They finally arrived back in Charing Cross Station on 29 December 1938 and immediately taken to St Stephen's Hospital, Fulham.

Despite the desperate attempts of the medical staff to save him, which included the removal of his left leg, the gangrene which had set in proved too far advanced, and Jimmy died on 7 January 1939, the last casualty of the Battle of the Ebro.[290]

Jimmy was buried in Milton Cemetery, Portsmouth, on 13 January 1939. Among those attending were his parents and brother and sisters, friends, workmates, representatives of the TGWU, Trades Council, Labour Party, and two returned Portsmouth British Brigaders, AC Williams and Stan Harrison. Among the wreaths was one whose inscription read, 'In memory of our gallant comrade who gave his life for the Spanish people in the cause of freedom and democracy'; from his 'pals' in the electrical shop and from his workmates.'[291]

Jimmy Moore as a boy, and his memorial stone—Courtesy of Joan Joslin

Chapter Nine

September 1938
The Last Stand of the British Battalion

On 21 September 1938 Spanish Prime Minister Negrín announced that it was his intention to withdraw the International Brigades from battle and arrange repatriation for those with a home to return to. By now the flow of international volunteers had slowed to a trickle, and their losses in battle had meant that the International Brigades were largely made up of Spanish soldiers, so their military importance was now minimal.[292]

Negrín hoped that this political gesture would ensure that international pressure would be put on Italy and Germany to withdraw their forces, and buy time until the now expected next World War began. He believed Spain would then get the planes and artillery it needed to even the odds against the fascists. His pleas continued to be ignored, and Franco duly triumphed at the end of March 1939, just a couple of weeks after Hitler had occupied all Czechoslovakia.

It is unclear whether the British Battalion were aware of Negrín's speech, although they had been expecting some sort of announcement about going home, having been moved into reserve positions. British Battalion Commissar Bob Cooney wrote that the company commanders and commissars were briefed but not the rest of the battalion.[293] He said that, 'We were going for our last fight on Spanish soil . . . We could not help but speculate on our chances of coming out alive. It was a cruel test, but not a man wavered. The last battle of our battalion was as glorious in its heroism and self-sacrifice as the first great stand at Jarama.' He was referring to the fact that, on the night of 21/22 September, the Fascists launched another offensive and were threatening to break through the Government lines at Sierra del Lavall de la Torre.

The XIII International Brigade had suffered terrible losses and the XV were called up to relieve them. With the American Lincoln Battalion on the right, and the Canadian Mac-Paps on the left, the British Battalion had to face the full force of the Fascists once again. Bill Alexander recalled that 'when the Battalion moved up on the night of the 22 September its strength was 377, of whom 106 were British. When it withdrew on the night of the twenty-fourth it was 173 strong, of whom 58 were British. Two hundred men were killed, missing or taken prisoner'.[294] However, as at Jarama, they held the line.

Roy Theodore Watts (1913-1938)

Roy Watts – Courtesy The Leicester Mercury, 6 October 1938

Roy Watts was born at home, at 35 Alpine Road, Hove, Sussex, on 13 September 1913, the son of a hairdresser's clerk. After school he went to work for the Portsea Island Mutual Co-operative Society. He led a full and active life; as well as his work, he was a member of the Shop Assistants Union, and represented the Portsmouth Branch on the Executive Committee of Portsmouth Trades Council.[295] [296] He was also elected Vice-President of the Southern District Council of NAUSAWC, and became an active member of the Young Communist League where 'one of his many and varied activities in the working class movement was addressing meetings on Southsea Seafront in the summer of 1936'.[297] [298]

His first taste of direct action against fascism was, along with his friend Fred Hill, attending 'a huge meeting at a local Portsmouth theatre being addressed by Mosley.'[299] The pair of them threw leaflets over the balcony and because Roy was seated next to the gangway he was seized upon by the 'stewards' and rough-handled down the long staircase having his coat ripped in the process'.[300]

In addition to his other activities he also enjoyed sport being the Chairman of the Portsmouth & District Clarion Cycling Club and was a 'well-known swimmer, holder of several trophies.'[301] [302] Sometime in the second half of 1936 Roy moved to Leicester and worked as a salesman in the furnishing department of the Leicester Co-operative Society.[303]

Roy arrived in Spain on 14 February 1938 and, despite being a very fit young man, the overnight journey over the Pyrenees left him with a fever which necessitated an immediate spell in hospital. Of his decision to go to Spain he wrote to a friend, 'The fight of the Spanish workers is also our fight and because the peace of the world is at stake I am happy to be able to show to the Spanish people, by my example, that, although our Government has hindered them, we in the working class are solid in support. Victory for the

Spanish people means that democracy and peace shall advance and flourish throughout the world.'[304]

The Secretary of Portsmouth Trades Council received a letter from Roy in April 1938 in which he outlined the challenges faced by the Spanish Government, 'I now know of the terrible sacrifices and hardships our fellows and the Spaniards are undergoing. I know too that if the people and comrades at home were faced with the same realisation they would redouble their efforts to help . . . most of the food we can get is rice or rice bread. A substantial piece of even donkey or mule flesh would be a real luxury. However, milk for the children in the big cities is really an urgent necessity.' [305]

He further wrote, 'Just now the war situation is very vital, and I can assure you that German and Italian intervention has made this war highly mechanised. The superior number of planes, tanks and arms etc. is a very decisive factor in its outcome. The farce of non-intervention now prevents the Spanish Government from buying arms.' Despite this realistic assessment of how the war was progressing he remained optimistic saying, 'The country is a beautiful one—mountains, olive groves, orange trees etc. It is also so rich in possibilities, and, until now, so oppressed by feudal landlordism, that you can sense that immediately the war is successfully concluded a tremendous progress and development will take place within a very short period.'

Having already served in the British Battalion infantry, and anti-aircraft unit, Roy was transferred to the Brigade Transmissions Unit on 22 June 1938. His final battle was described by Peter Kerrigan in a letter to Harry Pollitt dated 27 September 1938.[306] [307] [308] 'The irony of it is that this last action took place on September 23, the day after Dr Negrín's speech at Geneva which announced the repatriation of the volunteers . . . The Battalion had been in reserve position for 9 days, but what a reserve position! I saw them on one of the only two days when they had complete quiet. All the rest of the time they were under continuous artillery and aviation bombardment. One bomb dropped on a small house where our transmissions were, and killed Joseph Harding of Middlesbrough and Roy Watts of Leicester along with two Spanish comrades. When the bodies were dug out all were dead.'[309]

News of the withdrawal of the International Brigades would have been high on the agenda when Leicester Communist Party met in the Secular Hall on the evening of the 5 October 1938, so it must have been shocking for all attendees when the Chairman announced he had just been told that Roy Watts had been killed. Certainly it was all the more devastating for Roy's girlfriend, Phyllis Rowe. The local paper reported, 'when the message was read Miss Rowe was greatly distressed, and was taken home by fellow members of the Young Communist League.'[310]

George Robert Greig Burton (1916-1989)

George Burton was born in the family home at 74 Kilmiston Street, Landport, Portsmouth on 2 April 1916, the son of a Stoker Petty Officer in the Royal Navy. After school he worked as a salesman for the Portsea Island Co-op Society in Portsmouth and became a member of the Co-op Party and the Amalgamated Union of Shop Assistants, Warehousemen and Clerks.[311] One of his work colleagues was Roy Watts, who may well have been influential in politicising him, and in his decision to go to Spain. George arrived in Spain on 16 June 1938, one of the last of the British volunteers to go.

He was in No 2 Company of the XV International Brigade, and on 25 July transferred to Brigade Transmissions, reuniting with Roy Watts. Apart from three weeks suffering from dysentery he spent the whole period on the Ebro front, until the International Brigades were withdrawn on 23 September.[312] The notes on his record from Battalion HQ were not particularly flattering, but this was no doubt not helped by the fact he was 'non-party.'[313]

George was repatriated with the bulk of the British Battalion in December 1938, and returned to Portsea Island Co-op as manager of the Furniture Department in Fratton Road.[314] His life then took another dramatic turn when he joined the Palestinian Police, as British Constable no 76, on 22 October 1939.[315]

At the end of the World War Two he returned to Southampton and boarded a boat, on 14 May 1946, to Mombasa, in Kenya, where he worked for the British Government in an unknown role, and also ran a cattle ranch. While in Kenya he met and married German born Brigitte Hanse, and in 1965 they migrated to Canada, where they had a son. During his time there his jobs included working in a pulp mill.[316] George passed away on 3 January 1989, in Nanoose Bay, British Columbia, Canada.

George Burton – Courtesy of Keith Burton

Ivor Rae Hickman (1914-1938)

Ivor Hickman was born in 24a Gordon Avenue, Southampton on 6 September 1914. His father, a collector for a gas company, responded to the call to arms and, as a Corporal in the Machine Gun Corps won the Military Medal in 1917 for 'gallantry and example in the field'.[317] Sadly, he died prematurely as a result of his experience on the Western Front. Ivor's mother remarried in 1924 and the family moved to Dunster, in Somerset, taking over the Foresters Arms public house, by which time Ivor had won a scholarship to Peter Symonds Secondary School in Winchester, as a boarder.

Ivor played a full part in life at the school, not least in the Cadet Corps where he soon made the rank of Company Sergeant Major. The enthusiasm with which he went about everything he did is evident in the 'Musketry Reports' he wrote for the school magazine, with detailed assessments of the Company's progress, and exhortations to his fellow Corps members to go on to greater things.[318]

The Lent Term of 1933 also saw him take on the role of producer of the famous play 'Journey's End', the school's first dramatic production for a number of years.[319] As well as producing the play, he also took the lead role of Stanhope, which he played with 'power and realism'. The verdict on the production was that his 'work was as splendid in his inspiration of the play as a whole, as in his personal performance; to his unflagging enthusiasm and resource the success of the production may be largely attributed.'[320]

All this extracurricular activity was not at the expense of his academic work however, as he won several scholarships, including an Open Scholarship in Natural Sciences at Christ's College Cambridge.[321] His humble beginnings certainly did not inhibit him when it came making his mark at Christ's College. The famous novelist, C P Snow, a Fellow of the College at that time, noted how 'he was a man of singular charm, good nature and human warmth. He was liked by most people at first sight; he enjoyed life so much that one found it difficult not to do the same in his company, even if at one period in his undergraduate career the sight of his shock of fair hair coming around the door meant an interminable discussion on the meaning of meaning'.[322] He also continued his interest in the military and spent three years in the Officer Training Corps at Christ's, an experience which allowed him to a make an important contribution in Spain.

After graduation in June 1936 he moved to Manchester to take up a job with Metropolitan Vickers Electric Company which, according to C P Snow, would probably have led to a career involving research in metallurgy.[323] In December of the same year Ivor married Juliet Macarthur, in Manchester. They had met in Cambridge where Juliet, whose family home was on the Bedales School site in Petersfield, Hampshire, had been a student of Newnham College. After graduating as a teacher, she later became an educational psychologist.

Another relationship he continued after his time at Cambridge was an extraordinary friendship with the philosopher Ludwig Wittgenstein, who had been one of his lecturers. In response to a letter from Wittgenstein in October 1936 Ivor details the positive and negative sides of being a new engineering apprentice, along with the challenges of living in digs, and missing the intellectual stimulation he got from the lectures at Cambridge. He also wrote just before his marriage reminding Wittgenstein that he had met Juliet and his mother in Cambridge, and hoping that he would be able to visit at some time in the future.[324]

Ivor had joined the Communist Party in December 1935 whilst at University, and despite the beginning of a promising career, and deep love for his new wife, he could not ignore the fight against fascism in Spain.[325] He and Juliet made one last trip together to Paris, before he left her and made the arduous trip to Spain, crossing the Pyrenees overnight.[326] He entered

Spain on 10 October 1937, and most of the details we have about his time there are taken from the detailed and descriptive letters he wrote home to Juliet.[327]

He was certainly under no illusions about the task and dangers in front of him. From the training base at Albacete one of his first letters to Juliet recorded how, 'the military aspect fascinates me. Naturally I am afraid of the idea of going to the front, but when I look round and see many of my comrades I am damned glad I've had the military experience and interest that I have had . . . They simply won't face the fact that they will be dead if they don't learn here. I am sure that the mass of men don't realise what they are in for. They believe that political morale is enough—is it hell! You never heard of political morale turning aside a bullet.'[328]

Ivor & Juliet passport photos
Courtesy of Sarah Rhodes & Janie Shepherd

Ivor was made a sergeant and put in charge of a platoon, whilst anticipating a transfer to the Anti-Tank Battery. However, this was pre-empted by a move to the Officer Training School (OTS), the records showing that he had been recognised for his, 'All round technical ability and military experience. Should develop after work among men. Destined for big job in Spain. Cool.'[329] He was well aware that his first class education and lifestyle meant that there was something of gulf between himself and most of the other volunteers, he wrote to Juliet that he wished he 'wasn't so noticeably "University"/Comrade Hickman BA!'[330] However, at the OTS he also wrote that he, 'was much happier here at the school than I was in the company because I am being very well instructed (with certain gaps) and because there is somehow more common ground between us all here.'[331]

The OTS was also one of the very few places that allowed volunteers from different countries to spend time together, rather than being confined to their own national battalions. In particular Ivor found himself 'outgrowing his bias for Americans'. One particular friend was Albert Foucek from Nebraska who he found to be 'intelligent, easy to talk to and he doesn't philosophise'.[332] After graduating second in his class, Ivor was made Chief of Instructors at the Training School in Tarazona, commanding a variety of nationalities, including several African American comrades from the American Lincoln Brigade one of whom, Andrew Mitchell, was his Adjutant.[333] This highlighted how neither class nor colour was allowed to cause division amongst the volunteers, where all men were genuinely treated as equal. Many of the African American volunteers who survived the war were later to remark how their time in Spain was the best period of their lives, free of prejudice and enjoying mutual respect, despite the many dangers involved in war. A Spanish battlefield was also the bloody stage for the first time that a black American officer was to lead a mainly white battalion into battle, when

Oliver Law led the Lincoln Brigade over the top at Brunette, where he was killed.[334]

By the end of March 1938 Ivor had got his wish, and was sent up to the front with the Anti-Tank Battery, a vital section of the Battalion, but a relatively safe posting compared with the infantry companies. However, that was to change after the reorganisation made necessary by the losses incurred after the Fascist offensive through Aragon. He was promoted, to his great delight, to the position of observer with the British Battalion. It meant operating in the most dangerous of forward positions trying to map out enemy positions. He explained to Juliet that, 'it involves missions independent of the main body, which means more scope for initiative and more concentration.'[335]

On 24 July the Battle of the Ebro began with a surprise attack which saw great early success in terms of territory gained and prisoners taken. Sadly, the lack of adequate numbers of planes and heavy artillery to support the infantry, soon brought the advance to a standstill. It left the British battalion bogged down outside Gandesa, making several futile and costly attempts to take the notorious Hill 481, which saw the death of Ivor's friend and fellow observer, David Guest on 28 July.

The British Battalion was pulled back into reserve positions on 6 August and Ivor wrote to Juliet the next day describing his experiences, which included, 'observing the enemy at close range, being sniped, being shelled, attending staff meetings and thieving the Brigade Commander's delicious peaches, being shelled at night in a deserted village. Not boring exactly, but I hate it all. I shaped up pretty well— surprised myself, wasn't too afraid of shells and mortars. And was goddam cautious, I did not risk my life unnecessarily once. Because I have my life to complete, my life to live with you, my beautiful love.'[336]

He also offered reassurance in a letter to a friend saying,

'I'm very cautious and I don't believe in recklessness; nor am I brave, but I try to observe properly, which is to see but not to be seen. Observers get more artillery and more avions than the infantry, but the infantry gets the filth and the machine guns.'[337]

The list of citations for bravery in the British Battalion recount a slightly different story than that told by Ivor, as his name is mentioned twice.[338] Firstly, for the action on Hill 481, his citation reads, 'His work was of the highest merit and remained at his observation post during the fiercest bombardments and to whom is due the perfection of the Battalion observation services.' For the final action on 23 September the citation reads, 'Chief of Observers. For efficient work, coolness and bravery under fire.'

His first citation was mentioned in an article in the Daily Worker of 24 August 1938, something he brushed aside in what would prove to be the last letter that Juliet would receive, written on 31 August 1938.[339] Perhaps rather prophetically he also wrote, 'Tomorrow will bring in September! And you seem to make September a limit. Well we'll see what September holds for us! Let's hope it will mean we will see each other again? Nothing like hope.'[340]

On 3 September a new fascist offensive began on a wide front including the Valle de Torre and the Sierra de Cabals. There was initial success as they were held, but they continued to make best use of their overwhelming superiority in planes and artillery. On 21 September Spanish Prime Minister Juan Negrín announced his intention to withdraw the International Brigaders from combat and arrange their repatriation. He naively hoped that this would lead to international pressure on Germany and Italy to also withdraw their forces in order to even the odds on the battlefield. However, the opposite was the case, and the fascist offensive was renewed. With a threat of a fascist breakthrough around Sierra de Lavall de la Torre the British Battalion were thrown into battle one final time. They held the line but, yet again, at a terrible cost. When the roll was called two days later, less than half the Battalion were present to respond to their names.

Ivor was not among them. It is not clear exactly how he died amongst the carnage and chaos of those last two days, but Battalion political commissar Bob Cooney recorded that he 'was killed by almost the last bullet of the day while reconnoitring the enemy positions.'[341] To add to Juliet's grief, Ivor was initially posted as wounded and put on a list of Brigaders preparing for repatriation, just as Herbert Fisher had been. She had taken a flat in Mornington Crescent, London, to await his return, only then to learn the worst possible news.

C P Snow concluded Ivor's obituary by writing, 'There is nothing to add to his own words, except what would have surprised him to hear said. He was a man of rich and generous humanity. He was a brave man who died for what he believed was right. This modern world of cowering masses is poorer by a man.'[342]

Chapter Ten

Medical Aid

The heroism of the International doctors and nurses who went to Spain, alongside their Spanish comrades, equals that of the soldiers. Along with trying to terrorise the civilian population through indiscriminate bombing, Franco also did the same to medical facilities. A Red Cross attracted bombers rather than deterring them. The topography of the Spanish terrain along with poor roads and a shortage of transport, meant that the best chance a wounded soldier had of survival was to receive initial treatment as close to the front line as possible, before a difficult trip to hospital. This simply added to the dangers the medical staff faced, but they were not discouraged.

Margaret Duncombe Finley (1913-2003)

Margaret Finley was born by the sea in Ryde on the Isle of Wight, on 22 December 1913. Tragically, her mother died from Addison's disease when she was just nine, and with her Post Office Overseer father struggling with four young children, she was largely brought up by two 'maiden aunts.'[343] Margaret first trained as a nurse on the Isle of Wight, and then later moved to London's King's College Hospital for a more formal training between 1933-36. This was followed by surgical training at the Royal Masonic Hospital in 1937-38.

After attending an Aid Spain rally in the East End, she decided to volunteer to go to Spain, arriving on 11 May 1938. She served as a nurse in Mataró, about 20 miles north-east of Barcelona, until 9th December, having formally joined the

British Battalion in August.[344] She continued to work in some very miserable and fairly unsanitary conditions, and later spoke of the terrible injuries that many soldiers had suffered. However despite the challenges, she obviously made a good impression, being described as confident and professional in her work, and trying to have good relations with her patients.[345]

Along with a group of young Spanish socialists and injured International Brigaders, she made her way to the frontier at Le Perthus, France, and from there was repatriated to the UK. Margaret left behind a young man she had become very close to, Enrique Moret Astruells, a sculptor and captain in the Spanish Republican army. When Catalonia fell to the fascists in January 1939 he was detained in Olot, but managed to escape across the Pyrenees where he was interned in the French concentration camp at Le Barcarès.

Meanwhile Margaret had embarked on a nationwide speaking tour of the UK with other British Brigaders, including two other nurses, raising money for Spanish refugees. Speaking to a large audience in Hull, she described the work of her medical unit, and the effects that non-intervention was having on the wounded and the general population. She said, 'When we left Spain we did not cease fighting. We merely changed out frontiers and are now fighting for the Spanish people in England now.'[346] Speaking to a similar audience in Cambridge she said, 'No political belief entitled us to stand aloof from this slaughter of innocent women and children.'[347]

She travelled to France early in 1939 and worked for the British Committee for Spanish Refugees. Somehow she found Enrique and sprung him from the camp, and they went on to Paris where they were married, although this cannot be verified. Mixing in left-wing and artistic circles, Margaret began to develop a growing interest in artists and art whilst also lobbying hard for the rights of the refugees,

She also became involved with the 'Dominicanización de la frontera' initiative launched by the Dictator of the Dominican Republic Rafael Trujillo, which encouraged European immigration. He pursued an open door policy admitting Jewish immigrants in the 1930s when most countries were turning them away. After the Spanish Civil War he promoted the immigration of the exiles, taking in some 5,000 refugees from the Spanish Republic.

Margaret arrived in the Dominican Republic in 1940, having sailed on the 'Cuba', a chartered steamship from Marseilles which was full of Spanish refugees. She found that conditions in the Dominican Republic were abhorrent, little better than the French camps that the travellers had been in and there was soon discontent. With her British passport, Margaret secured work with a committee helping to rehouse the refugees. As the conditions in the Dominican Republic worsened the couple relocated to Cuba in 1942, where Margaret secured work in the Anglo American Hospital in Havana.

Margaret Finley – Courtesy of Di Margetts

Enrique was working as a sculptor, but could not obtain a visa to enter the US, so Margaret took some of his works to New York and set up an exhibition. She never returned to Cuba, and in 1945 they were divorced and Enrique quickly remarried. Still in New York, Margaret obtained work with art curator Mildred Constantine as an agent for Latin American artists, sending money to the Spanish refugees when she could.

In 1946 Margaret returned to the UK to visit her family, where she was asked by the fledgling United Nations to be their Latin American Secretary. She travelled to post-war Czechoslovakia, where she met Jan Masaryk, the country's president, and then travelled back to Cuba to start a tour of Latin America. Unfortunately, she contracted hepatitis, and after suffering bouts of illness in Guatemala and Mexico, the trip was abandoned and she returned to New York, where she was hospitalised.

In 1947, after her recovery she was invited to a party in New York where she met Jan Schreuder, a Dutch cartographer and part time artist working for Shell in Ecuador. They married and she returned with him to Ecuador, where she encouraged him to take up painting full time. They bought a small studio in Quito and encouraged Ecuadorian Indians to develop their arts and crafts skills. They also set up the Casa de Cultura in Quito which was the first art gallery in Ecuador. Many of the traditional designs still seen in the markets were reintroduced by Jan and Margaret. She had become a competent artist herself but as she said: 'There was only ever room for one artist and ego in the household'.

In 1959 Jan was offered a job in the US at a university in Oklahoma, but Margaret was refused an entry visa because of her 'communist' background. Due to Jan's bad health they had to leave the altitude of Ecuador and, with his comfortable company pension, they moved to Spain where they became friends of Gerald Brenan, the Hispanist and member of the Bloomsbury Group. He recommended a house in Mijas to them, which they bought, later adding a plot of land nearby where they designed a house with a studio. Jan died there in 1964 but Margaret remained in the same house until her death on 5 September 2003.

Dorothy Clara Rutter (1907-1997)

Dorothy Rutter was born in Bayswater Row, Leeds, on 23 May 1907. By 1911 the family of seven children had moved to Park Terrace in Lower Parkstone, Poole, Dorset, close to her mother's family home, where her father had found a job as a theatre attendant.[348] [349] After attending local schools, Dorothy befriended Jenny Mills, the wife of a Baptist minister in London, and went to a theological college in Edinburgh to train as a missionary. However, she was sent away after a severe bought of pneumonia, and it was thought she would not be strong enough to be a missionary. So, in 1932, Dorothy moved to the Royal Free Hospital in London, where she spent three years training as a nurse, qualifying by examination in November 1935. She then took a job in a nursing home in Paignton, Devon.[350]

Possibly more through a sense of adventure than politics, Dorothy left for Spain in February 1937, choosing to leave quietly so as not to worry her mother. After an arduous trip to Spain in a donated ambulance, sustained only by 'bread and vermouth', she arrived in time to witness the results of the horror of the Battle of Jarama.[351] Unlike many of the other medical personnel Dorothy became politically committed enough to enlist with the International Brigades, and stayed with the British Battalion, and the 35th Division, until their repatriation. She served on all the fronts including the battles that followed Jarama, at Teruel, Belchite and the Ebro.

In August 1937 Dorothy and the rest of her team were moved to set up a mobile hospital at La Puebla de Hijar, near Quinto, just behind the front from where the Aragon offensive was to be launched. They turned four wooden huts, with no electricity or water supply into a hospital.[352] The pressures they experienced are described in the Spanish Medical Aid Bulletin, October 1937. From a 'frontline hospital on the Belchite Front . . . 160 operations were carried out in twelve days in an operating theatre that was little more than a shed, besides handling several hundred other cases . . . Dorothy Rutter worked night and day . . . They ate and slept, when they could snatch a few minutes, out in the open, or, if on duty for twenty or thirty hour stretches they lay down in the wards so they could be ready at a minutes notice'.[353]

As part of his strategy to terrorise and destroy his enemy, Franco deemed hospitals legitimate targets, and it was not unusual for Spanish Republican and international doctors and nurses to be bombed and strafed while they worked. Dorothy described one such raid which occurred just after she had finished a night shift and was accompanying a Spanish nurse to find a safe place to sleep.[354] Shortly after settling down in a cave a lot of local people poured in, and then the planes came, 'and suddenly there was the dreaded shrieking whistle of bombs falling through the air. Crash, Boom. I remained as flat as possible on the floor, the beating of my heart accelerated by the thought of us all probably in a moment torn limb from limb by a violent death dealing bomb . . . This bombing of the villages had been going on for the four days that I had been on night duty and I had not been able to snatch more than a brief sleep. That day I was all in and felt that whatever happened I must sleep.'

After checking in at the hospital she 'fell asleep below a huge rock, just in a hollowed out pit that took my mattress, myself and a few blankets.' And then the planes returned and began strafing, 'I put the mattress half over me and put the pillow on my head . . . and waited . . . The heavens and all the mountains seemed to be coming down on my head.' As the planes returned yet again she was joined by legendary Catalan surgeon Moises Broggi who had also been working all night.

'The surgeon lay still with eyes closed, exhausted. Yet I knew that later, after dusk, he would get a short sleep and a cup of coffee, then begin with another night of operating'. After the raid was over, they ran back to the hospital fearing the worst and found 'the tents were rifled and torn and in the operating theatre an American nurse, Helen Friedman, had been wounded by machine gun bullets from an aeroplane. A Spanish nurse was hit in the back and an American anaesthetist had a broken leg from shrapnel . . . In the ward the nurse on duty, Ada Hodson, an English girl, was wounded in the wrist and above the eye. Though the blood was trickling down her face she refused treatment until she had finished giving sedatives to all the patients. This nurse was very brave and we are all proud of her.'

Dorothy Rutter and Dr Broggi – Courtesy of Lorraine Savory

Attractive and vivacious Dorothy featured in many of the pictures of medical staff in Spain, and was clearly popular with her comrades. American nurse Esther Silverstein described her disposition as 'sunny' and that the 'patients loved her, as well they might.' Esther also recounted how Dorothy kept a small grey rabbit in her uniform pocket explaining that 'if the patient was busy looking at the rabbit perhaps changing his dressing was less painful.'[355] Probably one of the most iconic pictures of the medical aid teams is that of Dorothy receiving a tea urn from Keith 'Andy' Andrews at the back of an ambulance.[356]

Medical staff were the only internationals present when the Spanish Republican Army took Teruel on 17 December 1937. However, when the counter offensive began in January the 35th Division were moved up in support. Dorothy and her team were 'stationed in a village so near the fighting that severe wounds were treated within an hour.'[357] There was the constant sound of artillery from a short distance away and the ever present danger from daily air raids. In addition, the nurses were also called on by British Doctor Reggie Saxton to donate their blood directly into a patient, a process still very much in its infancy. Winfred Bates recounted how she 'saw them work for twenty-four and thirty-six hours at a stretch.[358] One of the patients was particularly delighted when Dorothy Rutter went on duty. I asked her why. 'I nursed him before, when he was wounded on another front' she said.'[359]

In July 1938 all the British medical personnel were relocated to Mataró to support the British Battalion at the Battle of the Ebro. A huge hospital able to accommodate 14,000 men was erected and it was here that Dorothy fell for the charms of William James (Bill) Harrington, although it is quite possible that they had met before after he was wounded on another front.[360]

Bill was born in London on 2 April 1915. A complex and Machiavellian character he was a self-confessed 'jack of all trades.'[361] He claimed to have been an aviator, seaman, sparks, journalist, fishmonger and poet.[362] It is unclear how much is true, a conclusion obviously reached in Spain with a note on his file saying, 'Unreliable politically, rather wild in statements for which under certain suspicion.'[363]

He had gone to Spain and joined the new British Battalion in January 1937, then fought at Jarama, after which he had a long spell in hospital with glandular problems. He was then on the front line at Belchite, Caspe and Gandesa where his leadership and bravery had earned him the rank of Sargento (Sergeant). He again returned to the front at the Battle of the Ebro, where he was wounded in the attack on Hill 481. The wound to his right knee resulted in four months in hospital, the last three being at Mataró.

It is possible that Bill and Dorothy went through a civil marriage ceremony in Spain, although all of these were later annulled by Franco and not recognised by the British Government. They were both repatriated in early December 1938, and went to live at Bill's family home in Thornton Heath. Croydon, Surrey. Bill left to take part in the tour of Britain with other returned British Brigaders and nurses, to raise money and awareness about Spain. At some stage Dorothy studied for her industrial certificate and went to work as a nurse in munition factories during World War Two, utilizing her considerable experience of looking after people with blast injuries.

Although a son was born to them in April 1940, the relationship broke down. Bill virtually disappeared, and the only records of him since then are a single entry on the electoral roll at his parents' home in Thornton Heath, Croydon, and a report that he worked for Ferranti Photography in Edinburgh in the late 1950s and early 1960s. It is believed that he may have been a ship's writer in the Navy during WW2.

After the war Dorothy returned to Torquay, Devon, where

she ran her own nursing home. It was there that she met and married Ronald Fryer, a former Major in the Gloucester Regiment, who worked at the home as her secretary. To escape rationing and post war Britain, they went to Australia in 1947 where they had their first daughter. In 1950 they moved to New Zealand where they had a second daughter, and Ronald joined the NZ army. However, they became homesick and returned to UK in 1955 where Ronald re-joined the British army.

After serving around the world, Ronald retired from the army in 1966, and the family returned to the UK from Germany and settled in Richmond. After a very happy marriage Dorothy was devastated when Ronald died in 1971 and, with her life almost turning full circle, she returned to Bournemouth to be near her roots and her remaining sister. She had always considered Bournemouth home, and it is there she died in April 1997.

Henry Saunders Bury (1913-1993)

Dr Harry Bury was born on 13 February 1913, in Ashley Bridge, Bolton. His father was a Baptist Minister who took on the role of Padre to troops in France during the First World War. In 1918 he obtained a ministry in Pokesdown Baptist Chapel in Bournemouth, and the family lived in nearby Southbourne.[364] Traumatised by what he had seen in the war Harry's father decided to give up the ministry; and he entered a government scheme for ex-servicemen, taking on a smallholding in Holdenhurst, Bournemouth.

After going to school locally, Harry went to London to study for his premedical exams at King's College in the Strand, from there he went on to King's College Hospital. He became secretary of the Socialist Society for a time, and also joined the Communist Party. Along with other members of the Socialist Society he was often to be found at protests against Mosley and his British Union of Fascists, setting up first aid posts to deal with those who had been injured by the fascist thugs and the police.

After six years of study Harry qualified as Doctor in July 1937, and he began to think about going to Spain. He had observed the rise of fascism across Europe and in England, and determined that 'Spain was seen to be the last hope we had of stopping fascism and the threat of European war.' He applied to the Committee for Spanish Medical Aid to be sent to Spain but was told that he needed more experience before he would be permitted to go.

After a six month spell as a Surgical Houseman at the Belgrave Hospital for Children, he was permitted to go to Spain and left from Victoria Station on 1 May 1938, accompanied by two nurses returning after leave, Margaret Powell and Nan Green. Just a week after arriving in Spain he was posted to a hospital near Gerona, called Farners de la Selva, which had been turned into a base hospital for many of the casualties from the battles around the Ebro River.[365] The medical team were as representative of the world as the International Brigades themselves, and included three English nurses, Aileen Sparling, Mary Slater and Janet Robertson. Tragically, an outbreak of typhoid would later claim the lives of Mary Slater and Janet Robertson, and Harry was also struck down for a time with a severe bout of dysentery.

These illnesses were in no small part due to the conditions caused by the Non-Intervention Treaty which led to a lack of basic medical equipment, drugs, x-ray machines, and even food. This placed a terrible strain on all the medical staff, but also led to some great innovations such as the development of blood transfusions by Canadian Doctor Norman Bethune, and British Doctor, Reggie Sexton. Harry was particularly interested in Catalan Surgeon, Dr Trueta's method of encasing shattered limbs in plaster. Flesh wounds were left undressed and, in the absence of anti-biotics, maggots were left to keep the wound clean until the bone had healed and it was time to remove the plaster. As well as tending front line casualties Harry and his team were also treating injuries resulting from Hitler and Mussolini's bombers, particularly children, many of whom lived in an orphanage in the town.

After the last battle involving the British Battalion at Sierra Caballs on 23/24 September 1938, and the subsequent withdrawal of the International Brigades, Harry's patients were evacuated to Barcelona, and he was sent to join the remnants of the British Battalion at Ripoli. As well as tending those wounded in battle, there were typhoid cases and the ongoing battle with lice. After the bulk of the Battalion had been repatriated back to the UK, Harry, the nurses, and other medical personnel stayed behind for another two weeks before boarding a train that had been adapted to an ambulance with sixty nine sick and wounded.[366]

It was a long, bitterly cold journey, and a shortage of blankets that left some patients with frostbite. The increasingly exhausted medical team continued to treat them as best as they could. After stopping in Paris, a number of the most desperately ill, including Jimmy Moore, were left behind at the Hartford British Hospital to try and stabilise their condition before going home. The rest continued on to Victoria Station in London where they were greeted by a large cheering crowd, and three ambulances took the fifteen worst cases to the Middlesex Hospital.

Harry stayed overnight with friends in Bloomsbury and returned home to Bournemouth the next day. After recovering from his ordeal, he found a position as Senior House Surgeon at the municipal hospital in Lewisham, London. This post was followed by periods as a locum including a spell at Great Yarmouth, which led to another position assisting the Local Medical Officer for Health. He was put in charge of the infectious diseases hospital, dealing with tuberculosis, diphtheria, whooping cough, and other diseases which were often fatal amongst poorly housed and ill fed working class children. The impending World War also hastened a decision to marry Dorothy Hodgson, who he had first met through the Inter Hospital Socialist Society.

Dr Harry Bury – Courtesy of Victoria Razak

In 1940 Great Yarmouth hospital was evacuated due the danger of air raids, and Harry was appointed as an Assistant Medical Officer of Health in the West Riding of Yorkshire, responsible for school medical and child welfare services. Then, in October 1942, he was finally called up by the army and joined the Royal Army Medical Corps. He spent the war largely stationed in Scotland and India, and was finally demobbed in May 1946.

After his experiences in public health before the war he decided that 'preventing ill health made much more sense than treating it.' With that in mind he enrolled in the London School of Tropical Medicine and Hygiene in order to get a

Diploma in Public Health. The family home in Bournemouth, 'Squirrel Bank.' was sold, and after splitting the proceeds with his brother, Harry was able to purchase a house in Hampstead to accommodate his growing family. He continued his involvement in politics throughout this time, including selling the Daily Worker outside the local underground station on Saturday mornings.

Having passed his Diploma, Harry was given a position back in the West Riding of Yorkshire, soon moving to become the Medical Officer for Health in Saddleworth. He re-joined the Socialist Health Association and took part in the campaign to explain the benefits of the new National Health Service to the public. In 1952 he moved to a job as District Medical Officer of Health for Bedfordshire. During this period vaccines for polio and TB became available, along with an increased understanding of the industrial processes which caused working class people so much ill health. New friendships also resulted in Harry attending all the early Aldermaston Marches to protest against nuclear weapons.

In 1966, his marriage now having failed, Harry took on his final position as a Medical Officer for Health in Shropshire. He later remarried to Gladys, and lived a busy life in retirement in Shrewsbury. This included attending various events organised by the International Brigades Association, and being reunited with comrades from Spain. From 1984 he was also an active member of the International Physicians for the Prevention of Nuclear War, since renamed as Medical Action Against Nuclear Weapons, and in 1985 he had the honour of being one of five British doctors to represent the organisation when it received the Nobel Peace Prize in Oslo.

Harry died of lung cancer on 18 December 1993. An obituary recorded that following an incident as a child, 'he was cursed for his excessive ardour, but he went on being ardent about his chosen causes until his death at the age of 80.'[367]

Chapter Eleven

Hampshire's Aid to Spain

The ambivalence, and even tacit approval in some quarters, of the Tory Government and the majority of the press towards the threat of fascism in Spain, was widely disapproved of across the country. Aid to Spain Committees sprang up in towns and cities across the UK, raising money for food and medical supplies, along with increasing pressure on their elected representatives to end the arms embargo on the democratically elected Republican Government.

Typical of the resolutions of support was one passed by Southampton Trades Union Council, tabled just two weeks after the coup d'état began. It read, 'This meeting, representative of 30,000 citizens of Southampton, heartily congratulates the Government and people of Spain on the heroic resistance they have maintained against the brutal and unprovoked attack of the fascist bandits. It assures them of the whole-hearted support of the working class members of Southampton in their magnificent struggle for liberty and justice.'[368]

The response from W Craven-Ellis, one of Southampton's Conservative MP's was quite telling in how it highlighted the Conservative Party's attitude towards fascism at the time. He parroted the pro-Franco lie that it was actually the democratically elected Spanish Republican Government which was the 'greatest possible enemy to democracy', and that supporting one side or the other 'might easily produce a first class war'. In pushing the idea that it was all a big Communist conspiracy he added that 'recently Germany and Italy came to an understanding and this has established an anti-communist barrier, for which we should be grateful.'[369]

Although the Labour Party was very slow to actively support the Spanish Government, and to oppose the Non-Intervention Treaty, this was not mirrored in local Wards and Constituencies across the country. In September the Southampton Trinity Ward Women's Section heard an address by Councillor Mrs M Cutler, who said that 'all Socialists sympathised with the Spanish workers who were defending, with their blood, the principle of political democracy.'[370]

This was a view also echoed in a meeting of the Winchester Socialist League, who were 'convinced that the only method by which the Fascist offensive in Europe can be checked is by an extension of the Franco-Soviet Pact to include Britain . . . it therefore urges the Labour Party to demand that the Government takes this course before giving its consent to the Government's Re-armament Policy.'[371]

Legendary Trade Union leader, Tom Mann, then addressed a packed audience of 2,000 people at a meeting organised by Southampton Communist Party, in the local Coliseum Hall.[372] Having recently returned from Spain he condemned the Government's 'sham neutrality,' and urged the TUC and Labour Party to pressure the Government to 'assist the workers and democrats in Spain in their fight against Fascism.'[373] A meeting of staff and students at University College, Southampton also agreed a resolution which noted that the Non-Intervention Treaty has 'meant that the Spanish Government has been unable to buy essential supplies while the rebels have been aided by the Fascist powers, supported by Portugal.'[374] They declared that 'the attitude of the British Government has been equivocal throughout . . . and it raises the suspicion that it desires the overthrow of the Spanish Government.'[375] Left wing firebrand Sir Stafford Cripps MP then addressed a meeting in the Connaught Hall, Southampton, at the invitation of the Winchester Branch of the Socialist League.[376] He said 'there was ample evidence that the Labour Party was not giving a lead to the movement for helping Spanish workers.'[377]

The next Labour MP to address a meeting in Southampton was David Grenfell, a Welsh miner, who had just returned from a visit to Spain. He spoke in Chantry Hall and gave graphic details of the suffering of the Spanish people under the constant bombing from German and Italian planes.[378] He said, 'If non-intervention could be made effective there is no doubt that the Spanish Government would win. As it was the situation in Spain was an invasion of the country by Germany and Italy rather than a civil war.' The meeting was also significant as it was the first gathering since the death of Ray Cox had been relayed back home. Alderman Tommy Lewis asked the meeting to stand in silence and to remember a 'young man who gave his life for the sacred cause of liberty.'[379]

The General Committee of Southampton Labour Party, to which Ray had been a delegate, then met and passed a strongly-worded resolution calling on the British Government to get an assurance from the German and Italian Governments to abide by the Non-Intervention Treaty. Local Labour heavyweight Ralph Morley said that 'it was high time that the bluff of Hitler and Mussolini was called, and preferably by our Government. It is our duty to ensure the victory of the democratic forces in Spain.'[380] As a contrast to passing resolutions, practical help was also being organised and local branches of the Women's Co-operative Guild and Labour Party were busy knitting garments to help battle the fierce Spanish winter. These were 'sent to Spain through the London Spanish Relief Committee.'[381]

There was an obvious contrast in the way that events in Spain, and the support for the Republican Government in Hampshire, were reported in the County's daily papers. The editorial line of the Daily Echo in Southampton was unenthusiastically supportive of the British Government's policy of non-intervention, but there was always room in the paper for news about meetings and events to support the Republican cause. In stark contrast the News in Portsmouth vehemently supported non-intervention, and gave plenty of room for a couple of correspondents in particular, who were happy to laud the exaggerated claims made by the fascists. The weekly papers generally prioritised reports on whatever was happening outside Southampton and Portsmouth. This included meetings of Mosley's British Union of Fascists which had a degree of support in the County. One such meeting was held in the Lower Albert Hall in Portsmouth, where the main speaker, Alexander Raven Thompson described Fascism as the enemy of democracy, a silly outworn creed . . . pointing to Germany as the country where true liberty had been obtained through action.'[382] Southampton also had its supporters of fascism. The Municipal election of 1937 brought out 'Alfred Gipson as the first ever fascist candidate to stand in Southampton. He contested the St Mary's Ward in the City, regarding the election as good propaganda for the movement.'[383]

The first annual dinner of Eastleigh Labour Party, in the local Town Hall, attracted a lot of coverage as a result of being graced with the presence of Clement Attlee, the Leader of the Labour Party. Attlee attacked the National Government for standing by while countries were suffering under Hitler and Mussolini. He 'asked what we are supposed to get out of the betrayal of Abyssinia and Spain and for giving all kind of advantages to someone who, so far as I know, has never shown any desire to keep any promise . . . It is a tradition in this country that democracy is a British institution. Today, everywhere in the world, attempts are made against democracy, and the people of the world are looking to us for a lead.'[384]

In January 1937 the National Unity Campaign was formed. It was an attempt to bring all left wing political forces together to present a united front in the battle against

133

fascism. This resulted in three of the biggest names in British politics holding joint meetings in the southern Hampshire railway town of Eastleigh and Southampton during March 1937. Public meetings were held in the Town Hall in Eastleigh, and in the Coliseum and Atherley Hall in Southampton.[385] They were addressed by Sir Stafford Cripps as Leader of the Socialist League, Scottish Communist MP Willie Gallacher, and Fenner Brockway for the Independent Labour Party.[386]

It was not just in the largest centres of population in Hampshire that residents were organising to help Spain. The market town of Petersfield's Spanish Relief Committee put on a showing of the film 'Defence of Madrid' in their local Town Hall.[387] The Portsmouth Left Theatre Club also put on a performance and a collection was made, to be shared between the Spanish Medical Relief Fund, the Spanish Youth Food Ship, and dependents of those killed in Spain.[388] In the east Hampshire town of Alton, at the Assembly Room, the prospective Labour candidate for East Hampshire spoke of his recent experiences during a visit to Spain.[389] Ellen Wilkinson the Labour MP for Jarrow spoke to a meeting organised by Romsey Labour Party in the town's Abbey Hall. She said that 'we can no longer think of the next war as something that is going to happen, it has already begun . . . We have to realise that there is a new menace in the world, something called Fascism.'[390]

Local Labour parties continued to pass resolutions calling for an end to the non-intervention policy which was denying the Republican Government the planes and artillery they so desperately needed. Southampton Labour Party passed such a resolution, along with another expressing their condolences to the parents of Harold Laws who had been killed at Teruel.[391] This was followed up by a Sunday evening meeting on Southampton Common under the heading of 'Save Spain— Save Peace'. Labour Parties and Trade Unionists from the

Test Valley town of Romsey, the cathedral city of Winchester, and Lymington in the New Forest were represented along with other areas. Alderman Tommy Lewis explained that the 'objects of the demonstration were to show the solidarity of Labour and their sympathy with the Spaniards in the magnificent fight they were putting up for freedom, not only for themselves, but also for the workers of the world.'[392]

Fundraising events to fill the foodships for Spain were held in every part of Hampshire and the Isle of Wight, including a flag day in Alton which was opposed by the Fascist prospective candidate for East Hampshire who 'supplied a counter attack by organising a parade of leaflet distributors in the town.'[393] In Portsmouth, free use of the Guildhall was granted by the City Council for a dance to raise funds. This was part of a 'Spain Week' which included a flag day across the city which raised £83. Contributions of food were also made, including 1,000 tins of milk from Ryde and other parts of the Isle of Wight. Events in Bill Alexander's town of Ringwood included a film show, whist drive, and jumble sale.

The final accounts of the Hampshire Foodship for Spain show an audited figure of £2,734 which bought a sizeable contribution of food and other supplies. These were loaded on to the 'SS Stanleigh' when it docked in Southampton on 16 March 1939. Despite knowing that Spain may well have fallen to the Fascists by the time it docked in Valencia, it was agreed that the humanitarian relief was desperately needed and should still be sent. The committee agreed to continue to fundraise with the proceeds to be split between helping to fund refugees' ships to Mexico, the home for Basque children in Moorhill, Southampton, and the British Battalion's Wounded and Dependents Aid Committee.

There is no doubt that Hampshire can be proud of its contribution in the war against Fascism in Spain. Whether it was contributions in money or in kind towards helping to fill the foodships, welcoming the Basque children to the UK, or travelling to face the enemy on a Spanish battlefield, ordinary people were resolute in their solidarity and support of the Spanish people.

Within months it was Hampshire's turn to prepare to face the bombs and bullets of Hitler and his Nazis. Emboldened by the lack of opposition from the Governments of Britain, France, and America to their exploits in Spain, they unleashed their well-practiced bombers over the likes of Southampton and Portsmouth. It would take another six years and millions of deaths before Fascism was defeated. A terrible price to be paid for 'non-intervention'.

"Franco Sends Bombs, We Send Milk"
Spanish Aid Collection, Fratton, Portsmouth
Courtesy of Joan Hill

Selected Bibliography

Achier, Marcel, ed. *From Spanish Trenches*. Modern Age Books, New York, 1937.

Adams Eddie; Moreno Juan; Santana, Alonso; Tyler, Maggie; ed. *Echoes of Spain, Volunteers and Refugees Reminiscence Group on behalf of Echoes of Spain Group*. Gloucester Court, 2008.

Alexander, Bill. *British Volunteers for Liberty: Spain 1936-1939*. Lawrence and Wishart Ltd, London, 1982.

Alexander, Bill. *No to Franco. The Struggle Never Stopped 1939-1975*. Bill Alexander, London, 1992.

Alexander, Sally; Firth, Jim. *Women's Voices from the Spanish Civil War*. Lawrence and Wishart, London, 1991.

Baxell, Richard. *Unlikely Warriors: The British in the Spanish Civil War and the Struggle Against Fascism*. Aurum Press Ltd, 2012.

Baxell, Richard. *British Volunteers in the Spanish Civil War*. Warren & Pell, 2007.

Beeching, William C. *Canadian Volunteers. Spain 1936-1939*. Canadian Plains Research Center, 1989.

Bell, Adrian. *Only for Three Months: The Basque Children in Exile*. Watkiss Studios Ltd, Biggleswade, 1996.

Bridgeman, Brian. *The Flyers*. Self-Publishing Association, Upton-upon-Severn, Worcs, 1989.

Brown, Lorne. *When Freedom Was Lost*. Black Rose Books, Montreal, 1987.

Buchanan, Tom. *The impact of the Spanish Civil War on Britain*. Sussex Academic Press, 2007.

Bury, Henry Saunders. *Medicine, Politics and War*. CENDA, Buffalo, New York, 1993.

Cloud/Kapp, Yvonne. *The Basque Children in England*. Gollancz, 1937.

Cooney, Bob. *Proud Journey: A Spanish Civil War Memoir*. Marx Memorial Library and Workers School & Manifesto Press, 2015.

Croft, Lisa. *Activists: Lessons from my Grandparents*. 2015.

Currie, Roz; Hahn, Susan; Jump, Meirian. *Islington and the Spanish Civil War*. Marx Memorial Library & Workers School, Islington Council, 2017.

Deegan, Frank. *There's No Other Way*. Toulouse Press, Liverpool, 1980.

Derby, Mark, ed. *Kiwi Compañeros: New Zealand and the Spanish Civil War*. Canterbury University Press, New Zealand, 2009.

Farman, Chris; Rose, Valery; Woolley, Liz. *No Other Way. Oxfordshire in the Spanish Civil War 1936-1939*. Oxford International Brigade Memorial Committee, 2015.

Foote, Alexander. *Story of a Russian Spy (Handbook for Spies)*. Hillman Periodicals Inc. 1949.

Fyrth, Jim. *The Signal Was Spain: The Aid Spain Movement In Britain 1936-1939*. Lawrence and Wishart, London, 1986.

Gascoyne, David. *Journal 1936-1937*. The Enitharmon Press, 1980.

Gates, John. *The Story of an American Communist*. Thomas Nelson and Sons, New York, 1958.

Graham, Frank. *XV International Brigade: Records of British, American, Canadian and Irish Volunteers in Spain 1936-1938*. Warren and Pell, 2003.

Guest, David. *A Scientist Fights for Freedom*. Lawrence and Wishart Ltd, London, 1939.

Gurney, Jason. *Crusade in Spain*. The Readers Union, Newton Abbot, 1976.

Hall, Christopher. *'Disciplina Camaradas': Four English Volunteers in Spain 1936—39*. Gosling Press, 1994, reissued in 1996.

Hall, Christopher. *In Spain with Orwell: George Orwell and the Independent Labour Party Volunteers in the Spanish Civil War 1936-1939*. Tippermuir Books Ltd, 2019

Hartwell, Herbert and Evelyn. *The Long Weekend: A Working Class Couple's Involvement in the Spanish Civil War*. Post Mill Press, 1989.

Inglis, Amirah. *Australians in the Spanish Civil War*. Allen and Unwin, 1987.

Jackson, Angela. *For Us it was Heaven: The Passion, Grief and Fortitude of Patience Darton from the Spanish Civil War to Mao's China*. Sussex Academic Press, Eastbourne, 2012.

Jackson, Angela (Foreword and afterword). *Firing a Shot for Freedom: The Memoirs of Frida Stewart*. The Clapton Press, London, 2020.

Jump, Jim. *Poems from Spain*. Lawrence and Wishart, 2006.

Kingsford, Peter. *The Hunger Marches in Britain 1920-1940*. Lawrence and Wishart, London, 1982.

Langdon-Davies, John. *Behind the Spanish Barricades*. Martin Secker & Warburg Ltd, 1936; republished by The Clapton Press, 2022.

Laws, Herbert. *Forty Years with the Co-op*. Southampton Cooperative Society, 1951.

Liversedge, Ronald. *Mac-Pap: Memoir of a Canadian in the Spanish Civil War*. New Star Books, Vancouver, 2013.

MacDougal, Ian, ed. *Voices from the Spanish Civil War: Personal Recollections of Scottish Volunteers in Republican Spain 1936- 39*. Polygon, Edinburgh, 1986.

Molumphy, Henry, D. *For Common Decency: The History of Foster Parents Plan 1937-1983*. Foster Parents Plan International Inc, 1984.

Monks, Joe. *With the Reds in Andalusia*. Published by the Author and Distributed by The John Cornford Poetry Group, 1985.

Palfreeman, Linda. *Salud! British Volunteers in the Republican Medical Service During the Spanish Civil War*. Sussex Academic Press, 2012.

Percival, Bill. *The Great Explosion at Faversham 2 April 1916*. Reprinted from Archaeologia Cantiana Vol. C, 1985.

Petrou, Michael. *Renegades: Canadians in the Spanish Civil War*. Warren and Pell, 2008.

Romilly, Esmond. *Boadilla: A Personal Account of a Battle in Spain.* McDonald and Co, London, 1971. (First published 1937, Faber and Faber. Republished by The Clapton Press, 2018).

Scott, Thomas Gilbert. *A New Forest Childhood 1903-1916.* Cudworth Press, Ilminster, 2003.

Sloan, Pat, ed. *John Cornford: A Memoir.* Borderline Press, Fife, 1978.

Sommerfield, John. *Volunteer in Spain.* Lawrence and Wishart, 1937.

Spender, Stephen. *World Within World.* St. Martin's Press, New York, 1994.

Tinker, Frank Jnr. *Some Still Live.* Clapton Press, London, 2019.

Wainwright, John, L. *The Last To Fall: The Life and Letters of Ivor Hickman—An International Brigader in Spain.* Hatchet Green Publishing, Southampton, 2012.

Watson, Keith Scott. *Single to Spain.* Arthur Barker, London, 1937. Republished by The Clapton Press, 2022.

White, Allen. *Christchurch Airfield: 40 Years of Flying 1926-1966.* Allen White, Christchurch, Dorset, 1987, reissued 2005.

Notes

[1] Otherwise known as the Franco-Belgian Battalion.

[2] *Volunteer in Spain*, Lawrence & Wishart, 1937, pp 111-112.

[3] *The Good Comrade: Memoirs of an International Brigader*, Jan Kurzke, The Clapton Press, 2021.

[4] *From Spanish Trenches: Recent Letters from Spain,* edited by Marcel Acier, Rumfold Press, 1937, pp 75.

[5] For more details on Maclaurin and other New Zealanders who went to Spain see *Kiwi Compañeros: New Zealand and the Spanish Civil War,* edited by Mark Derby, Canterbury University Press, NZ, 2009.

[6] For more information about British Brigaders see *Unlikely Warriors: The British in the Spanish Civil War and the Struggle Against Fascism*, Richard Baxell, Arum Press, 2012.

[7] *John Cornford: A Memoir*, edited by Pat Sloan, Borderline Press, 1978, p 239.

[8] This biography of Ray Cox is largely an adaption of the eulogy given by his nephew, Steve Cox, at the unveiling of the Southampton Memorial bearing Ray's name on 28 October 2006.

[9] *The Great Explosion at Faversham, 2 April 1916,* by Arthur Percival. Reprinted from Archaeologia Cantiana Vol C, 1985, p 452.

[10] Formed in 1894 and named after The Clarion socialist newspaper, edited by Robert Blatchford.

[11] Southern Daily Echo, 28 December 1936.

[12] Tom Mann (1856-1941)—very popular Trade Union leader, socialist and public speaker.

[13] Ernst Thaelmann (1886-1944)—leader of the Communist Party of Germany. One of the first people to be thrown into a concentration camp when Hitler came to power in 1933. Murdered on Hitler's orders in 1944.

[14] Esmond Romilly (1918-1941)—nephew of Winston Churchill, eloped with Jessica Mitford before joining the International Brigades in Spain. They migrated to North America in 1939,

where he joined the Canadian Air Force. Lost on a bombing raid in 1941 over the North Sea. His memoir, *Boadilla* was published in 1937 and republished in 2018 by The Clapton Press.

[15] *Single to Spain* by Keith Scott-Watson, Arthur Barker, 1937, p 37. Republished 2022 by The Clapton Press.

[16] Thankfully the notebook survived as it also contains information about the individual members of the Centuria.

[17] Jaroslaw Dabrowski (1836-1871)—Polish revolutionary and republican. Died of wounds received on a barricade defending the Paris Commune.

[18] Tommy Lewis was Southampton's first Labour Councillor and served for around 50 years. Southampton City Council Archives D/TU1/2.

[19] Southampton MP from 1929—1931 and 1945—1950. (Source—Wikipedia).

[20] Ralph Morley was a renowned educationalist and an MP for Southampton from 1929-1931 and 1945-1955.

[21] Southern Evening Echo, 27 January 1937, p5. 'Died Fighting in Spain'.

[22] *Christchurch Airfield, 1926-1966, 40 Years of Flying* by Allen White, p 10.

[23] Christchurch Times, 3 October 1936, p 1. 'Killed in Spain'.

[24] *The Flyers* by Brian Bridgeman, pp 117-124. This remains the seminal work on British and International pilots who flew in Spain.

[25] Daily Express, 30 September 1936, pp 1-2. 'He Dies, She Must Go On In Ice Revue'.

[26] Christchurch Times, 10 October 1936, p 3. 'Back from the war pilots tell of local airman's death'.

[27] Daily Express, 10 October 1936, p 2. 'Bored by his money'.

[28] Portsmouth News, 7 December 1922, p 2.

[29] Portsmouth News, 30 September 1936, p 13.

[30] Portsmouth News, 12 October 1929, p 4.

[31] London Gazette, 15 January 1926, p 374.

[32] Hampshire Telegraph, 19 August 1928, p 18.

[33] Bridgeman, op cit, pp 115-130.

34 London Gazette, 6 January 1931, p 148.

35 London Gazette, 25 October 1932, p 670.

36 Portsmouth News, 12 June 1931, p 18.

37 Hampshire Telegraph, 15 December 1933, p 23.

38 Hampshire Telegraph, 1 September 1933, p 8.

39 Portsmouth News, 11 July 1935, p 5.

40 Portsmouth News, 22 October 1935, p 6.

41 Portsmouth News, 4 August 1936, p 8.

42 Bridgeman, op cit, p 122.

43 Ballymena Weekly Telegraph, 17 October 1936, p 9.

44 Daily Express, 30 September 1936, p 2.

45 Bridgeman, op cit, p.158-167.

46 National Archive KV5/129.

47 *Some Still Live* by F G Tinker jr, Funk & Wagnalls, New York, 1938, pp 23-25. Republished by The Clapton Press, 2019.

48 National Archives , FO 371/21296/187-190.

49 Portsmouth News, 17 February 1937, p 8.

50 Portsmouth News, 2 December 1944, p 6.

51 Bridgeman, op cit, pp 158-167.

52 NRO AIR/80/5/94. Helen Loveday Andrews spent a short time in the Women's Royal Air Force, being demobbed in November 1919.

53 National Records Office FO 371/21322/239-240.

54 The London Gazette, 18 January 1944, p 412.

55 The Navy, Army and Air Force Institutes which run recreational facilities and sell goods needed by service personnel and their families.

56 National Archives FO1060/1928.

57 *British Volunteers in the Spanish Civil War* by Richard Baxell, p 85.

58 Daily Worker, 23 February 1937, p 5. 'Workers Hero Dies in Battle'.

59 *Activists: Lessons from my Grandparents* published by Lisa Croft, 2015. Unless otherwise referenced all the information in this biography comes from this lovely tribute written by Lisa Croft to her grandparents, who opposed fascism and worked for

social justice all their lives.

[60] Star-Phoenix, 10 May 1933. 'Headed for Jail, Prisoners Chant Communist Song'.

[61] Star-Phoenix, 20 September 1934. 'Williams Blames Police Head For Trouble At Camp'.

[62] National Archives KV2/1611/76b.

[63] National Archives KV2/1611/50a.

[64] National archives KV2/1611/51w.

[65] After returning from Spain in September 1938 Foote was recruited to act as a spy for the Soviet Union, spying on the Germans, initially in Germany, and then from a base in Switzerland. After discovery he returned to the UK and was thoroughly interrogated by Special Branch. His extraordinary story is documented in the National Archives (KV2/1612/101c) and in a book he wrote, *Story of a Russian Spy. Handbook for Spies,* Hillman Periodicals, New York, 1949.

[66] For more detail of the involvement of the No 2 Machine Gun Company in the Battle of Jarama see *Unlikely Warriors* by Richard Baxell, pp 159-180.

[67] MML IBA Box 28/A/4.

[68] They heard nothing more until 1968 when, still employed at the ROF Bishopton, he and Jane Orme were summoned to Whitehall to be interrogated, 30 years after they were stolen. Much to his surprise, AC was questioned about the events and people whom he had written about in *Between Two Prison Gates.* Efforts were made to recover the manuscript from the Security Services, but in a letter to Mike Hancock MP, dated 4 September 2006 (Ref M19362/6), Security Minister Tony McNulty claimed AC's personal file had been destroyed in the late 1980's as part of a general clear-out and 'nor can they throw any light on the whereabouts of the memoirs'.

[69] National Archives KV2/1611/59a.

[70] National Archives KV2/1611/76b.

[71] The full name of the NPS was the National Amalgamated Society of Operative House & Ship Painters & Decorators. (1886-1941).

[72] The NUWM was set up in 1921 by members of the Communist Party of Great Britain in order to try and mobilise the huge numbers of unemployed workers throughout the UK, in particular against he Means Test.

[73] Portsmouth Evening News, 16 March 1937, p 2.

[74] RGASPI 545/6/89/10.

[75] Not to be confused with another British Brigader by the name of John Kelly, from Waterford, Ireland.

[76] I am grateful to his late daughter Annette Rigney for much of the detail of Jack's life before and after Spain.

[77] The ULTL was a Trade Union representing tailors in London. In 1939 it amalgamated with the National Union of Tailors and Garment Workers.

[78] MML IBA Box 39/A/23.

[79] *Journal 1936-1937* by David Gascoyne, The Enitharmon Press, 1980, p 7.

[80] The Times, 28 November 2001. Obituary.

[81] Ibid.

[82] Ibid, p 24.

[83] Letter to the author from Judy Gascoyne, February 10 2006. Judy had previously found fame of her own after being employed as the housekeeper to Bob Dylan and Beatle George Harrison at the 1969 Isle of Wight Rock Festival.

[84] Ibid, p 49.

[85] The seminal work on this remains *For Only Three Months. The Basque children in Exile* by Adrian Bell, Mousehold Press, 1996. See also the website of the BCA'37 UK for The Association for the UK Basque Children. www.basquechildren.org/

[86] National Archives FO371/21371.

[87] Ibid, pp 6-10.

[88] Hampshire Chronicle, 8 May 1937, p 2.

[89] *The Signal Was Spain. The Aid to Spain Movement in Britain 1936-39* by Jim Fyrth, pp 229-242.

[90] *The Basque Children in England* by Yvonne Cloud, Kapp Gollancz, 1937, pp 19-25.

[91] Southern Daily Echo, 15 May 1937, p 5. 'Getting Ready for

Basque Children'.

[92] Southern Daily Echo, 22 May 1937, p 1. 'A Cause Without Creed'.

[93] The fields were very close to where the huge Asda store, in Chandlers Ford, is now situated.

[94] Ibid, p 242.

[95] For the detailed history of Plan International see *For Common Decency. The History of Foster Parents Plan 1937-1983* by Henry D Molumphy, 1984.

[96] https://en.wikipedia.org/wiki/John_Langdon-Davies

[97] 'The Impact of the Spanish Civil War on Britain. War, Loss &Memory', by Tom Buchanan, Sussex Academic Press, 2006 p 141-157.

[98] National Archives KV5/126/1&2

[99] *Behind The Spanish Barricades* by John Langdon-Davies, Martin Secker & Warburg, 1936, pp 116-117.

[100] Molumphy, op cit, p 32.

[101] Email to author from David Williams dated 10 January 2006.

[102] Jim Fyrth wrote that Eric was a former Winchester school teacher and Indian cavalry officer, but he has probably confused him with another volunteer. Op cit, p 165.

[103] Letter to Walter Citrine, dated 3 January 1939. TUC archive, Ref 292/946/32/154, Warwick Digital Collection.

[104] Ibid.

[105] National Archives KV5/127 M.

[106] Molumphy, op cit, pp 36-44.

[107] Email to author from his grandson Jackson Towie dated 6 February 2022.

[108] Daily Mirror, 24 October 1968, p 9. 'Malcolm's Brother'.

[109] Scott, Thomas Gilbert, A New Forest Childhood 1903-1916, Culworth Press, 2003, p 31-33

[110] RGASPI 545/6/197, a short biography written by Humfry himself.

[111] Ibid.

[112] Gates, John, The Story of an American Communist, Thomas Nelson & Sons, 1958, pp 48.

[113] Monks, Joe, With the Reds in Andalusia, The John Cornford Poetry Group, 1985, p 33.

[114] Letter dated 30 April 1937. Courtesy of Elena Duran.

[115] RGASPI 545/3/440.

[116] Architectural Association (AA) Archives Box A502b.

[117] AA Archives Box A504.

[118] Portsmouth Evening News, 6 July 1933.

[119] National Archives ADM 196/171.

[120] After a number of mergers the Association became part of the Union of Construction, Allied Trades and Technicians (UCATT), which has now merged into Unite the Union.

[121] *Crusade in Spain* by Jason Gurney, Readers Union of Book Clubs, 1976, p 80.

[122] Ibid, pp 130-131.

[123] *World Within World* by Stephen Spender, Faber & Faber, 1951, pp 222-223.

[124] Dr Moises Broggi, a well-respected Catalan surgeon.

[125] MML SC/INDY/JFY/2/1/9.

[126] Details of his life before and after Spain provided by his nephew Mike Redman. Email to author, dated 29 June 2006.

[127] RGASPI 542/2/70/56.

[128] RGASPI 545/2/50/195.

[129] RGASPI 545/2/70/56.

[130] RGASPI 545/6/133/39.

[131] RGASPI 545/6/146/92. Letter dated, March 11 1938. She also claimed that he was encouraged to go to Spain with the 'promise of plenty of work'. This was patently untrue as volunteers who went via the Communist Party office in London were left under no illusions as to the situation they would be facing. See Baxell, *Unlikely Warriors*, pp 65-66.

[132] National Archives FO 889/2.

[133] RGASPI 542/2/53.

[134] RGASPI 545/6/53.

[135] The Cornishman, 28 September 1939, p 5.

[136] West Briton & Cornwall Advertiser, 21 September 1939, p 5.

[137] West Briton & Cornwall Advertiser, 28 September 1939, p 5.

[138] West Briton & Cornwall Advertiser, 21 September 1939, p 5.

[139] 'The Partido Obrero de Unificación Marxista' (POUM) were largely sympathetic to the political outlook of Leon Trotsky. This put them at odds with the communist led International Brigades and the Spanish Republican Government, which ultimately had fatal consequences for many.

[140] The ILP was positioned to the left of the Labour Party, to whom it was affiliated 1906-1932. The result of a split in 1932, and continuing internal political arguments, put the ILP into a slow decline as a political force. For the most comprehensive information about the ILP and its role in Spain see, *In Spain with Orwell, George Orwell and the Independent Labour Party Volunteers in the Spanish Civil War, 1936-1939*, by Christopher Hall.

[141] Western Daily Press, 22 October 1935, p 7. 'Bristol Captain's Death in Car Accident'.

[142] The Independent, 22 October 2011, Obituary: Stafford Cottman by David Keyes.

[143] *Disciplina Camaradas, Four English Volunteers in Spain 1936-39* by Christopher Hall, p 23.

[144] *Unlikely Warriors*, Baxell p 183.

[145] National Archives KV5/112-118.

[146] Ibid, pp 46-49.

[147] Ibid, p 47.

[148] Ibid, p 49.

[149] Ibid, p 113.

[150] The Independent, 22 October 2011.

[151] Uxbridge & West Drayton Gazette, 20 October 1999, p 20. 'A lifetime of politics'.

[152] *There's No Other Way* by Frank Deegan, Toulouse Press, 1980, pp 29-32.

[153] RGASPI 545/3/498/18.

[154] RGASPI 545/2/54/20.

[155] RGASPI 545/3/452/113.

[156] RGASPI 545/3/457/113.

[157] IBA Box D-7 File A/1.

[158] Information courtesy of his son Christopher, telephone conversation with the author, April 2006.

[159] With thanks to his late sister Sylvia Holley for the record of his MN service. Letter dated 9 April 2006.

[160] RGASPI 545/6/190. A short potted biography of his life before Spain, written by himself.

[161] Ibid.

[162] Portsmouth Evening News, 22 October 1936, p 5. 'Gosport Labourer Bound Over'.

[163] RGASPI 545/6/190. No doubt to be used in mitigation for one of his many court martials, Albert helpfully wrote down the details of his exploits in Spain from the time of arrival until around early 1938. In cross checking this with Battalion papers lodged in the Moscow archive it has been possible to write this with a good degree of accuracy.

[164] Portsmouth Evening News, 24 March 1937, p 5. 'Gosport Man Fights For Democracy In Spain'.

[165] Ibid.

[166] R W Robson, previously the Communist Party's London District Organiser, who was responsible for vetting potential volunteers and making sure they knew exactly what they were getting involved in *Unlikely Warriors: The British in the Spanish Civil War and the Struggle Against Fascism* by Richard Baxell, 2012, p 65,

[167] Portsmouth Evening News, 4 June 1937, p 8. 'Gosport Man Home From Spain'. The story was also reprinted in the Hampshire Telegraph & Post, 11 June 1937, p 20.

[168] Ibid.

[169] Portsmouth Evening News, 7 January 1938, p 5. 'Gosport Man in Spain'.

[170] Baxell, op cit, p 281.

[171] RGASPI 545/2/302.

[172] RGASPI 545/6/190.

[173] Labour History Archive (People's History Museum) Manchester, CP/Cent/Pers/01/01.

[174] RGASPI 545/6/95/20.

[175] NUPB&PW (1928-1975) merged into the Society of Graphical & Allied Trades (SOGAT).

[176] Guardian Unlimited, 14 July 2000, Richard Baxell: Bill Alexander obituary.

[177] RGASPI 545/6/47/34.

[178] *XV International Brigade, Records of British, American, Canadian, and Irish Volunteers in Spain 1936-1938*, Warren & Pell, 2003, p 234.

[179] RGASPI 545/6/89/38.

[180] *British Volunteers for Liberty, Spain 1936-39* by Bill Alexander, Lawrence & Wishart, 1982, p 161.

[181] Ibid, p 166.

[182] Ancestry, 1939 England & Wales Register.

[183] Guardian Unlimited, ibid.

[184] Labour History Archive, ibid.

[185] Communist Party of Britain (CPB). https://www.communistparty.org.uk/bill-alexander/

[186] *No to Franco, The struggle never stopped 1939-1975* by Bill Alexander, 1992, p 19.

[187] By 2000 nature had taken its toll and there were too few Brigaders left alive to sustain the work of the IBA. It was superseded by the International Brigade Memorial Trust (IBMT) in 2001, when members of the IBA, and members of the Friends of the International Brigades decided to merge to form a single organisation.

[188] Morning Star, 26 July 2000, p 4. 'Mourners bid farewell to veteran brigader'.

[189] Herbert wrote a book about the Southampton Co-op called *Forty Years with the Co-op. Recollections and Reflections.*

[190] Unless otherwise referenced all the information about Harry Laws has been kindly supplied by his nieces Henrietta Quinnell and Catherine Silman, from the family archive, they also gave the eulogy at the unveiling of the Southampton memorial.

[191] Peterborough Standard, 25 March 1938, p 14.

[192] Ibid.

[193] The letter was printed in the Oxford Gazette, March 1938, p 1.

'What it is like to be bombed'.

[194] Harold was killed on 17 February 1938 along with Frank O'Brien of London. *See Proud Journey. A Spanish Civil War Memoi'* by Bob Cooney (British Battalion Commissar), Marx Memorial Library & Manifesto Press, 2015, p 53.

[195] Southern Evening Echo, 14 March 1938, p 1. 'Sad News for Southampton Parents'.

[196] Left wing Labour MP who became Chancellor of the Exchequer in Attlee's post war government.

[197] MML SC/VOL/HFI/1/10.

[198] The Draconian (Dragon School magazine), April 1939, p 9290. Letter dated January 1935

[199] Ibid. Letter to Hugh Derry, dated November 1937.

[200] Ibid.

[201] In an undated letter home Herbert said that he was acting as a runner for his Company Commander, John O'Sullivan from Dublin. He was also lost during the retreats.

[202] National Archives FO371/24123.

[203] RGASPI 545/6/133.

[204] Daily Worker, 19 December 1938, p 6.

[205] *Comrades* by Harry Fisher, University of Nebraska Press. 1998, pp 184-185.

[206] Johnny Power commanded one of the British Battalion Companies. Harry knew him from his time with the Lincolns.

[207] Belfast Telegraph, 3 March 1937, p 5.

[208] National Archive KV5 112.

[209] RGASPI 545/6/105.

[210] RGASPI 545/2/263.

[211] The school was established in 1895 and demolished in 1977.

[212] NA MEPO 4/349/239.

[213] In 1986 Douglas gave an interview to the Imperial War Museum detailing his life through to his return from Spain. www.iwm.org.uk/collections/item/object/80018339.

[214] RGASPI 545/6/36/3.

[215] RGASPI 545/6/91/146.

[216] RGASPI 545/6/99/2 and 545/6/127/79.

217 RGASPI 545/3/451/156.

218 RGASPI 545/6/127/78.

219 NA KV5/112/E.

220 Email to author from Patrick Brady forwarding information from niece Diana dated 11 September 2021.

221 *Voices from the Spanish Civil War* edited by Ian MacDougall, Polygon, 1986, p 53.

222 RGASPI 545/6/193/38.

223 Dundee Evening Telegraph, 26 April 1945, p 4.

224 Dundee Evening Telegraph, 9 September 1947, p 1.

225 Bo'ness Journal & Linlithgow Advertiser, 27 April 1951, p 4.

226 Edinburgh Evening News, 1 March 1954, pp 4-5.

227 Dundee Courier, 3 June 1954, p 3.

228 Email to the author from his nephew Simon Theobalds, dated 18 February 2008.

229 West London Observer 15 November 1935, p 5.

230 The Daily Worker was the daily paper of the Communist Party of Great Britain, and the precursor of today's Morning Star newspaper.

231 RGASPI 545/3/456/34.

232 Ibid.

233 Echoes of Spain, the volunteers from Kensington, London. Compiled and edited by members of the Echoes of Spain Mosaic Group, p 17.

234 National archives, FO 371/24122 219-220.

235 RGASPI 545/6/40.

236 Daily Worker, 27 October 1938, p 1.

237 Between the two World Wars the Militia or Citizens Force was something of a cross between a Home Guard and the Army Reserve.

238 Ibid, p 1.

239 Belfast Telegraph, 26 October 1938, p 12.

240 *Australians in the Spanish Civil War*, by Inglis & Amirah, Allen & Unwin, 1987, pp 183-184.

241 I am indebted to John's son, Malcolm, for much of the detail about his father's life.

[242] *David Guest, A Scientist Fights for Freedom*, edited by Carmel Haden Gust, Lawrence & Wishart, 1939, p 17. The book is a collection of observations and testimonies from family, friends, and acquaintances, who had known David throughout his life.

[243] Ibid, p 29. Related by his brother Peter.

[244] Ibid, p 67.

[245] Liverpool Echo, 9 September 1931, p 5. 'Westminster Scenes'.

[246] Norwood News, 24 April 1936, p 4. 'Sunday Trouble on the Orators Ground'.

[247] Wessex News, Vol 4, No 1, 18 October 1938.

[248] Southern Evening Echo, 8 August 1938, p 3. 'MP's Son Killed in Spain'.

[249] Portsmouth Evening News, 22 March 1938, p 25. 'Portsmouth Youth Rally'.

[250] MML IBA Box 50/Gs/1.

[251] RGASPI 545/6/144/21.

[252] Norwood News, 16 September 1938, p 8.

[253] RGASPI 545/6/196/30.

[254] A comparison can perhaps be made with the Victorian workhouses in the UK, except they were for single, workless and homeless men. Forced to work under a strict regime and compulsory labour for a pittance. For the full story of the camps and the resistance that was formed see *When Freedom Was Lost* by Lorne Brown, Black Rose Books, 1987.

[255] RGASPI 545/6/196/30.

[256] RGASPI 545/6/568/27.

[257] For the full story of the Canadians in Spain see *Renegades: Canadians in the Spanish Civil War* by Michael Petrou, Warren & Pell, 2008.

[258] The battalion was named after William Lyon Mackenzie and Louis-Joseph Papineau the leaders of the rebellions of 1837 in Upper and Lower Canada.

[259] RGASPI 545/2/58/435.

[260] The role of the Brigade scouts in this battle was described by fellow Canadian scout Fed Mattersdorfer in *Canadian Volunteers: Spain 1936-1939* by William C Beeching, Canadian

Plains Research Center, 1989, pp 153-155.

[261] RGASPI 545/6/568/27.

[262] RGASPI 545/6/537/127.

[263] *Mac-Pap. Memoir of a Canadian in the Spanish Civil War* by Ronald Liversedge, New Star Books, 2013, p 154.

[264] Charles Gidora, CPBC, email to author dated 12 March 2007.

[265] Not to be confused with another Stanley Harrison who was a journalist, and later sub-editor, of the Daily Worker.

[266] This biography includes information from a number of documents that Stan Harrison wrote. It includes three questionnaires he completed in Spain (RGASPI 545/6/146/45-56), a letter he wrote to Bill Alexander (MML IBA Box 29/D/5), the story of his service in Spain (MML IBA Box 29/D/6), and a paper he wrote, on his family's history, for his daughter, Rosalyn, before his death in 1985, a copy of which she has kindly given to the author.

[267] David Brown Taunton's School archivist, email to author, 2 April 2007. Taunton's School has since evolved into Richard Taunton College.

[268] Historically, Trade Union Branches in the print industry have always been known as 'Chapels', and the Chairperson, the Mother or Father of the particular Chapel.

[269] Portsmouth Evening News, 17 December 1938, p 3. 'Portsmouth Men in Spain'.

[270] Portsmouth Evening News, 19 December 1938, p 3. 'Foreign Volunteers in Spain'.

[271] MML IBA Box 29/DD/5 dated 31 October 1984. By then Alexander was Chair of the International Brigade Association, which was set up both to ensure the lasting memory of the British Brigaders, but also to remind people why they went to Spain. The IBA became the International Brigade Memorial Trust. http://www.international-brigades.org.uk/.

[272] MML IBA Box 50/pt/3.

[273] Portsmouth Evening News, 21 January 1939, p 3. 'Arms for Spain'.

[274] GRO Alverstoke 1910.

[275] *The Long Weekend* by Herbert & Evelyn Hartwell, Postmill Press,1988. Every effort has been made to corroborate the events described in the book, as the mists of time, with the 50 year gap until publication, have meant some errors of recall.

[276] The NUWM was set up by members of the Communist Party to organise the mass ranks of Britain's unemployed between the wars, in order to gain publicity for their plight. *See The Hunger Marches in Britain 1920-1940* by Peter Kingsford, Lawrence & Wishart, 1982.

[277] RGASPI 545/6/150/68.

[278] Ibid.

[279] *The Lost Weekend* (p 14) incorrectly names him Harris Wendel and gives the year as 1937.

[280] RGASPI 545/6/98/5.

[281] In his book Herbert describes being involved and wounded at the battle of Teruel in January 1938 (p 30). As Teruel was over before his arrival in Spain it is possible he was confusing the events here with Aragon or the Ebro. The only questionnaire he completed, which is in the archives (RGASPI 545/6/150/68), is dated 12 April 1938. It mentions the Aragon conflict but not any wound.

[282] Ibid, pp 23-24.

[283] Ibid, p 40.

[284] RGASPI 545/6/174/6-12 dated 20th November 1938. Questionnaire completed whilst lying in his hospital bed awaiting repatriation to the UK.

[285] Ibid.

[286] Ibid.

[287] Portsmouth News, 9 November 1938, p 5. 'A Portsmouth Fighter in Spain'.

[288] National Archives, FO 369/2514/59. Although all the returning British Brigaders had to sign the form almost all of them refused to pay, and the Government had the good sense not to pursue the matter.

[289] *The Signal Was Spain: The Aid Spain Movement in Britain 1936-39'* by Jim Fyrth, Lawrence & Wishart, 1986, pp 134-135.

[290] Chelsea News & General Advertiser, 13 January 1938, p 3. 'Wounded in Spain. Young Man Dies at St Stephen's Hospital'.

[291] Portsmouth News, 14 January 1939, p 2.

[292] The International Brigades had always included a percentage of Spanish soldiers in order to make up the numbers to Brigade/ Battalion strength, but this greatly increased towards the end.

[293] *Proud Journey* by Bob Cooney, p 106.

[294] *British Volunteers for Liberty* by Bill Alexander, p 215.

[295] The National Amalgamated Union of Shop Assistants, Warehousemen & Clerks (NAUSAWC) merged into the Union of Shop, Distributive & Allied Workers (USDAW) in 1947.

[296] Portsmouth Evening News, 18 October 1938, p 2. 'Young City Man Killed in Spain'.

[297] Leicester Evening Mail, 5 October 1938, p 1.

[298] Ibid.

[299] Sir Oswald Mosley, leader of the British Union of Fascists.

[300] Letter to the author from the late Joan Hill dated 11 February 2008.

[301] Ibid.

[302] Ibid.

[303] The Leicester Mercury, 6 October 1938, p 13. 'Leicester Man Killed in Spain'.

[304] Co-operative News, 16 April 1938, p 3. 'Salesman Fights for Spain'.

[305] Portsmouth Evening News, 14 May 1938, p 7. 'Spanish War Experiences'.

[306] Leading British Communist and Daily Worker correspondent in Spain.

[307] MML IBA Box C:25/5.

[308] General Secretary of the British Communist Party, who visited the British Battalion on at least three occasions during the war.

[309] Juan Negrín (1892-1956), Prime Minister of the Spanish Republic from May 1937 to March 1939.

[310] Ibid, p 13.

[311] Now part of USDAW—Union of Shop Distributive & Allied

Workers.

[312] RGASPI 545/6/112.

[313] Members of the Communist Party of Great Britain made up about two thirds of the volunteers and the majority of the senior ranks.

[314] Email to the author from nephew Brian Burton, dated 27 June 2006.

[315] Email to the author from Graham Jenkins, Palestine Police Old Comrades Association, dated 24 April 2008.

[316] Email to author and conversation with his son Keith Burton, 6 November 2012.

[317] Hampshire Independent, 3 November 1917, p 4.

[318] Peter Symonds School Magazine, Lent term, 1932, pp 800-801. With thanks to Peter May.

[319] Written by R C Sherriff, it is set in an officer's dugout in First World War trenches in France.

[320] Ibid, pp 16-17.

[321] Peter Symonds School Magazine, Summer term, 1933, p 91.

[322] Christ's College Magazine, No 144, 1939, pp 47-49. With thanks to Katie Coakes, Alumni & Development Officer.

[323] Ibid, p 47.

[324] Letters dated 25 October 1936 and 29 November 1936. Courtesy of Professor Brian McGuiness.

[325] RGASPI 545/6/148.

[326] RGASPI 545/6/148/5.

[327] Juliet kept all Ivor's letters, and passed then on to her two daughters from her second marriage, shortly before her death in 1977. They remained stored and unread by anyone until contacted by the author in 2009, thanks to the assistance of Dennis Archer, the archivist at Bedales School, and Jean Moya, Juliet's younger sister. They can be read in full in a beautiful and moving account of Ivor's life in, *The Last to Fall. The life and letters of Ivor Hickman—an International Brigader in Spain* by John L. Wainwright, Hatchet Green Publishing, 2012.

[328] Ibid, pp 80-81.

[329] RGASPI 545/2/213/25.

[330] Ibid, p 104.

[331] Ibid, p 110.

[332] Albert Foucek was later killed at Gandesa during the retreats through Aragon on 3 April 1938.

[333] Andrew Mitchell was also killed at Gandesa, leading a training company to try and stem the advance of the Fascists.

[334] Oliver Law learnt his politics on Chicago's South Side, the same area which would later provide America's first black president, Barack Obama.

[335] Ibid, p 146.

[336] Ibid, p 188.

[337] Ibid, p 191.

[338] MML IBA, Box 21/B/7b.

[339] Daily Worker (the precursor to the Morning Star newspaper): 'British Heroism in Great Battle of Spain War'.

[340] Ibid, p 207.

[341] *Proud Journey* by Bob Cooney, p 107.

[342] Christ's College Magazine, p 49.

[343] Unless otherwise referenced I am indebted to Margaret's niece, Di Margetts, and a great friend and carer in the later years of her life, Lyn Armitage, for their emails to the author containing the details of her life.

[344] RGASPI 545/6/133/19.

[345] Ibid.

[346] Hull Daily Mail, 1 February 1939, p 3. 'Spain War through a Nurse's Eyes'.

[347] Cambridge Daily News, 7 February 1938, p 5. 'Spanish Republic Is Not Defeated'.

[348] Poole has always been located in Dorset, whereas Bournemouth and Christchurch were part of Hampshire until 1974 when they were moved into Dorset.

[349] I am grateful to Dorothy's daughter, Lorraine Savory, for the unreferenced information about her mother's life.

[350] General Nursing Council register of nurses, with thanks to Kate Mason, RCN.

[351] Daily Express, 12 March 1937, p 5. 'British Nurses in Spain

Send News. O.K.-Love'.

352 *The Signal Was Spain* by Jim Fyrth, p 96.

353 National Labour History Archive & Study Centre, CP/IND/Murp/01/01, Nurse Molly Murphy.

354 Woman Today, March 1939 , pp 19-20. 'War on Spanish Hospital' by Winifred Bates.

355 *Women's Voices from the Spanish Civil War*, edited by Jim Fyrth & Sally Alexander, pp 149-150. It should also be noted that, in note 45 to Esther's story (p 173) Dorothy is said to have been killed at Dunkirk, in World War 2—this is not correct.

356 Much loved and respected for his work as a 'chauffeur, anaesthetist, nurse and mother and father to them all', the story of Andy's life is beautifully told *in Soldier Saving Lives: Keith Howard Andrew* by Dave Chapple, Somerset Socialist Library, 2021.

357 Spanish Information Service. 'With the British and American Medical Aid at Teruel'. 11 February 1938, p 2. MML IBA Box 29/A/7b.

358 Winifred Bates was the wife of author Ralph Bates, and a journalist and broadcaster. She spent much of her time in Spain as something of a 'personnel officer' for the nurses, not only with her articles about their work but also making representations on their behalf back to London.

359 Spanish Information Service, p 2.

360 MML IBA Box 29/A/7. Report No 3, Barcelona, 4 August 1938, p 7.

361 RGASPI 545/6/146/24.

362 He certainly had talent as a poet. See *Poems From Spain*, edited by Jim Jump.

363 RGASPI 545/6/146/27.

364 Unless otherwise referenced the details of Harry's life are taken from *Medicine, Politics, and War* which he wrote and was published in 1993.

365 In 1939 it was renamed Santa Coloma de Farners.

366 RGASPI 545/6/112/65-77. Harry made a good impression in Spain. Comments about his work included, 'His work as a doctor

is very good, his professional conduct is perfect, very disciplined and respectful. Relates very well with the injured and with his comrades, very active in his cultural work.'

367 The Guardian, 13 January 1994, p 38. 'Harry Bury' by Bill Westall.

368 Southern Daily Echo, 30 July 1936, p 5. 'Labour's Message to Spanish People'.

369 Southern Daily Echo August 8 1936, p 5. 'Mr Craven-Ellis MP Replies'.

370 Southern Daily Echo September 14thy 1936, p 1 .

371 Hampshire Chronicle, 17 October 1936, p 1.

372 The Coliseum Hall was located in Portland Terrace, Southampton, and demolished in the 1960s.

373 Southern Daily Echo, 19 October 1936, p 5.

374 In 1952 it became the University of Southampton.

375 Southern Daily Echo, 23 November 1936, p 24. 'Supply of Arms to Spain'.

376 Located at 167 St Mary's Road, it was demolished to make way for a Six Dials 'road improvement' scheme around the 1970s.

377 Southern Daily Echo, 14 December 1936, p 5. 'Is Labour Supporting Re-Armament?'.

378 Chantry Hall was in St Mary's Street Southampton. Built in 1925, it was demolished soon after a 'mysterious' fire in 2007.

379 Southern Daily Echo, 2 January 1937, p 24. 'The Tragedy in Spain'.

380 Southern Daily Echo, 14 January 1937, p 5. 'German and Italian Troops in Spain'.

381 Southern Daily Echo, 29 January 1937, p 7. 'Help for Spanish Workers'.

382 Hampshire Telegraph & Post, 29 January 1937, p 18. 'Fascism at Portsmouth'. The Lower Albert Hall was in Commercial Road, Portsmouth and hosted a meeting at which William 'Lord Haw-Haw' Joyce was the main speaker on 7 December 1936. He was executed in 1946 for treason. Alexander Raven Thompson was a committed Nazi, and one of Mosley's top lieutenants. They spent the Second World War together in prison as suspected traitors.

[383] Southern Daily Echo, 23 October 1937, p 24. 'Southampton Fascist Candidate'. He polled 29 votes.

[384] Southern Daily Echo, 28 February 1937, p 5. 'Back to the Jungle Diplomacy'.

[385] The Atherley Hall was located in Howard Road, Southampton.

[386] The Socialist League was affiliated to the Labour Party, campaigning to move it to the left politically. It was soon proscribed by the Labour Party and dissolved itself in June 1937.

[387] The film was made in 1936 and showed how Madrid was defended in the early months of the year. The director was Ivor Montague, the second son of the second Lord Swaythling whose main home was Townhill Park House (now Gregg School) in Southampton. A renowned film maker, reviewer and champion table tennis player, he won the Lenin Peace Prize in 1959.

[388] Hampshire Telegraph & Post, 2 April 1937, p 9. 'Aid For Madrid'.

[389] Hampshire Advertiser, 3 July 1937, p 5. 'Prospective Labour Candidate at Alton'.

[390] Southern Daily Echo, 8 October 1937, p 7. 'Horrors of War in Spain'.

[391] Southampton Daily Echo, 24 March 1938, p 24. 'Spanish Arms Embargo'.

[392] Southern Daily Echo, 2 May 1938, p 5. 'Labour's May Day Celebration'.

[393] Hampshire Telegraph, 10 February 1939, p 10. 'Food Ship for Spain'.

ALSO AVAILABLE FROM THE CLAPTON PRESS

**WILD GREEN ORANGES, AN AUTOBIOGRAPHICAL NOVEL
by Bob Baldock**
1958. Sierra Maestra, Cuba. Two young Americans spend five months with Fidel Castro's combat unit, el Movimiento 26 de Julio. While there, the author became the only US citizen from the mainland to see action in combat with Fidel's guerilla unit. Written in the early 1960s, fresh from the jungle, this novel is based on those experiences and can now finally be released.

MY HOUSE IN MALAGA by Sir Peter Chalmers Mitchell
While most ex-pats fled to Gibraltar in 1936, Sir Peter stayed on to protect his house and servants from the rebels. He ended up in prison for sheltering Arthur Koestler from Franco's rabid head of propaganda, who had threatened to 'shoot him like a dog'.

**BRITISH WOMEN AND THE SPANISH CIVIL WAR
by Angela Jackson – 2020 Edition**
Angela Jackson's classic examination of the interaction between British women and the war in Spain, through their own oral and written narratives. Revised and updated for this new edition.

BOADILLA by Esmond Romilly
The nephew that Winston Churchill disowned describes his experiences fighting with the International Brigade to defend the Spanish Republic. Written on his honeymoon in France after he eloped with Jessica Mitford.

SOME STILL LIVE by F.G. Tinker Jr.
Frank Tinker was a US pilot who signed up with the Republican forces because he didn't like Mussolini. He was also attracted by the prospect of adventure and a generous pay cheque. This is an account of his experiences in Spain.

ALSO AVAILABLE FROM THE CLAPTON PRESS

NEVER MORE ALIVE: INSIDE THE SPANISH REPUBLIC
by Kate Mangan, with a Preface by Paul Preston
When her lover, Jan Kurzke, made his way to Spain to join the International Brigade in 1936, Kate Mangan went after him. She ended up working with Constancia de la Mora in the Republic's Press Office, where she met a host of characters including WH Auden, Stephen Spender, Ernest Hemingway, Robert Capa, Gerda Taro, Walter Reuter and many more. When Jan was seriously injured she visited him in hospital, helped him across the border to France and left him with friends in Paris so she could return to her job in Valencia.

THE GOOD COMRADE, MEMOIRS OF AN INTERNATIONAL BRIGADER
by Jan Kurzke, with an Introduction by Richard Baxell
Jan Kurzke was a left-wing artist who fled Nazi Germany in the early 1930s and tramped round the south of Spain, witnessing first-hand the poverty of the rural population, later moving to England where he met Kate Mangan. When the Spanish civil war broke out in 1936, Jan went back and joined the International Brigade, while Kate followed shortly after, working for the Republican press office. Many of his fellow volunteers died in the savage battles on the outskirts of Madrid and Jan himself was seriously wounded at Boadilla, nearly losing his leg. This is his memoir, a companion volume to *Never More Alive*.

IN PLACE OF SPLENDOUR: THE AUTOBIOGRAPHY OF A SPANISH WOMAN by Constancia de la Mora,
with a foreword by Soledad Fox Maura
Constancia de la Mora was the grand-daughter of Antonio Maura, who had served under Alfonso XIII as Prime Minister. She was one of the first women to obtain a divorce under the fledgling Spanish Republic. During the civil war she became a key figure in the Republic's International Press Office, moving to the USA and Mexico after the war was lost. This is her memoir, with a detailed history of the build-up to the conflict.

ALSO AVAILABLE FROM THE CLAPTON PRESS

SPANISH PORTRAIT by Elizabeth Lake
A brutally honest, semi-autobiographical novel set in San Sebastián and Madrid between 1934 and 1936, portraying a frantic love affair against a background of confusion and apprehension as Spain drifted inexorably towards civil war.

THE FIGHTER FELL IN LOVE: A SPANISH CIVIL WAR MEMOIR by James R Jump, with a Foreword by Paul Preston and a Preface by Jack Jones
Aged twenty-one, James R Jump left his Spanish fiancée in England and went to Spain to join the International Brigade. He was mentioned in despatches for bravery during the Battle of the Ebro. His previously unpublished memoir brings back to life his time in Spain and the tragic course of the war he took part in, while the accompanying poems reflect the intense emotions sparked by his experience.

FIRING A SHOT FOR FREEDOM: THE MEMOIRS OF FRIDA STEWART with a Foreword and Afterword by Angela Jackson
Frida Stewart drove an ambulance to Murcia to help the Spanish Republic and visited the front in Madrid. During the Second World War she was arrested by the Gestapo in Paris and escaped from her internment camp with help from the French Resistance, returning to London where she worked with General de Gaulle. This is her previously unpublished memoir.

STRUGGLE FOR THE SPANISH SOUL & SPAIN IN THE POST-WAR WORLD by Arturo and Ilsa Barea, with Introduction by William Chislett.
Arturo and Ilsa Barea worked for the Republic's Press and Censorship office in Madrid. After the civil war, they found refuge in the UK, where Arturo broadcast weekly bulletins to Latin America for the BBC World Service and continued writing. These two essays called on the democracies of Europe to unseat Franco, both falling on deaf ears. Together the two essays present a horrific picture of the early years of the dictatorship, which was to endure until Franco's death in 1975.

Ingram Content Group UK Ltd.
Milton Keynes UK
UKHW020839230423
420621UK00012B/1599